WEST SIDE STORY, the most popular musical drama of our time, both on Broadway and as a movie, is based on one of Shakespeare's finest tragedies, ROMEO AND JULIET. In this volume are both works, which, though separated by centuries, parallel each other in many ways.

NORRIS HOUGHTON, Professor of Drama at Vassar College and a co-founder of the Phoenix Theatre, has prepared the introduction for this volume. Mr. Houghton is the author of ADVANCE FROM BROADWAY, BUT NOT FORGOTTEN, MOSCOW REHEARSAL and RETURN ENGAGEMENT, and the editor of Dell's MASTERPIECES OF CONTINENTAL DRAMA SERIES, GREAT RUSSIAN SHORT STORIES and GREAT RUSSIAN PLAYS.

JOHN BETTENBENDER, who has provided extensive notes for ROMEO AND JULIET, is Professor of Drama at St. Joseph's College, Indianapolis, Ind.

ALSO AVAILABLE IN LAUREL-LEAF BOOKS:

WILLIAM SHAKESPEARE

ROMEO AND JULIET

WEST SIDE STORY

Book by ARTHUR LAURENTS

Music by LEONARD BERNSTEIN

Lyrics by STEPHEN SONDHEIM

Entire production directed and
choreographed by JEROME ROBBINS

Introduction by NORRIS HOUGHTON

Notes by JOHN BETTENBENDER

CAUTION: Professionals and amateurs are hereby
warned that WEST SIDE STORY, being fully
protected under Copyright Laws of the United
States of America, the British Empire, including the
Dominion of Canada, and all other countries of the
Berne and Universal Copyright Conventions, is
subject to a royalty. All rights, including professional,
amateur, motion picture, recitation, lecturing, public
reading, choreographic, radio and television
broadcasting, and the rights of translation into foreign
languages are strictly reserved. Particular emphasis is
laid on the question of readings, permission for which
must be secured from the author's agent in writing. All
inquires should be addressed to MCA Artists, Ltd.
598 Madison Ave., New York, N.Y. 10022.

Published by
Dell Publishing
a division of
The Bantam Doubleday Dell Publishing Group, Inc.
666 Fifth Avenue
New York, New York 10103
Copyright © 1965 by Dell Publishing Co., Inc.
Text of ROMEO AND JULIET reprinted by arrangement
with Harper and Row, New York, N.Y.
WEST SIDE STORY Copyright © 1956, 1958
by Arthur Laurents, Leonard Bernstein, Stephen Soundheim
and Jerome Robbins. Lyrics Copyright © 1957
by Leonard Bernstein and Stephen Soundheim.
Reprinted by permission of Random House, Inc.
The trademark Laurel-Leaf Library ® is registered in the U.S. Patent
and Trademark Office.
ISBN: 0-440-97483-6

RL: 5.9

Printed in U.S.A.
All rights reserved
September 1965
50 49 48 47 46
WFH

CONTENTS

INTRODUCTION

ROMEO AND JULIET and
WEST SIDE STORY: AN APPRECIATION

When young William Shakespeare sat down in the year
1594 to compose a play about a pair of teen-age "star-
crossed lovers," he based his story on a narrative poem he
had recently read, by a man named Arthur Brooke, called
The Tragical Historye of Romeus and Juliet.

When young Arthur Laurents sat down some 360 years
later to mull over an idea Jerome Robbins had been brood-
ing about for several seasons, it was to Shakespeare's play,
Romeo and Juliet, that he turned to base his *West Side
Story.*

Shakespeare, to be sure, had other sources for his theme
besides Brooke: there was the tale of Hero and Leander
in classic legend; there was Tristan and Yseult in medieval
lore. Indeed, it would seem as though poets had sung since
the world began of the tragedy of love thwarted by fate.
Laurents, too, had other and closer sources to draw on:
the saga of the Hatfields and the McCoys, to mention but
one. Indeed, the old saw that there is nothing new under
the sun applies to the stage as aptly as to any other area
of human endeavor. People are always rewriting other
people's stories—consciously or unconsciously—cutting and
trimming, pasting, rearranging, and adjusting to new times
and circumstances, sometimes adding truly creative elements and occasionally actually improving on the original.

Whether *West Side Story* does or does not improve upon
Romeo and Juliet it would be futile to discuss. What in-

terests us are the ways in which these two theatre pieces, separated by so many centuries, resemble each other, the ways in which they diverge, and to speculate on the reasons therefor.

As a rule, the texts of musicals make unsatisfying reading. They are skeletons that need music and dancing, color and light to flesh them out. *West Side Story* is no exception. As you read Stephen Sondheim's lyrics and Arthur Laurents' dialogue, you can hardly avoid hearing Leonard Bernstein's haunting music in your mind's ear and seeing Jerome Robbins' dynamic patterns of movement in your mind's eye; provided, that is, that you have been fortunate enough to have sat before them in performance on either stage or screen. In this instance, comparison of the contemporary play with its Renaissance predecessor forces one to remark that frequently its music and its dance pick up where its text leaves off, to lift it toward the heights of poetic rhapsody that Shakespeare's verse accomplishes unaided. Still, in this volume we have necessarily only words to read and talk about, so having made obeisance to the contributions of Bernstein and Robbins, let us now turn to this play and to Shakespeare's, considering them as dramatic works, looking first at the similarities.

The stories are, of course, the first thing that strikes one by their parallelism. The feuding houses of Montague and Capulet in old Verona have their counterpart in the rival gangs of New York's West Side. By introducing us into this feuding world through younger and lesser members of the gangs, Laurents follows Shakespeare, Sampson and Gregory becoming A-Rab and Baby John. Prince Escalus and his Veronese officers who break up the first street fight find their counterparts in Officers Krupke and Schrank. In both plays the atmosphere of violence and hate, uneasily held in check by authority, is quickly established. So, too, is the youthfulness and impetuosity of the world of both. It may be helpful to try to think of Benvolio and Tybalt, Mercutio and Romeo as scarcely older than Bernardo and Chino, Riff and Tony, even though the former are not often played by teen-age actors (though perhaps they should be!).

Once the environment has been established, each play moves quickly to the first confrontation of the young lovers-to-be, taking time only to introduce them to us separately first. Romeo, we find, is already lovesick for a girl we shall never know—Rosaline. He moons for her:

> Tut, I have lost myself; I am not here.
> This is not Romeo, he's some other where,

he explains. Tony, although he has no specific girl, stands waiting to love:

> The air is humming
> And something great is coming!
> Who knows?

And as he waits, the gang loses his interest: "Riff, I've had it," he says, as though to say, "This is not Tony, he's some other where."

Next we meet Juliet and Maria, Juliet with her mother and her nurse, Maria with her girl friend, Anita, who is also her brother's girl. Maria is the intended of Chino; Juliet also has a suitor, Paris. And now two things must be remarked. First, that Laurents has increased his heroine's age slightly. At fourteen girls may have been betrothed and wed in the sixteenth century; in ours it stretches credulity. Nevertheless, he takes care to establish that Maria is younger and more innocent than the other girls surrounding her. Second, there are no adult members of the household in *West Side Story,* no counterparts to old Capulet, Lady Capulet or the Nurse, no elder Montague or Lady Montague either. The grown-up world seems far more alien to the youngsters of Laurents' play than to those of Shakespeare's. We hear of Tony's mother and of Maria's Mama and Papa, but only in passing. The officers of the law, a shadowy settlement-house worker nicknamed "Glad Hand," and Doc, the drugstore proprietor, are the only adults in *West Side Story.* Cut off from sympathetic relationships with the elder generation, the Sharks and the Jets have only each other; their suspicion of grown-ups and alienation from them may contribute to the tragedy.

The Capulet ball has its obvious parallel in the settlement-house dance. As more than three hundred years before, boy and girl—now Polack and Puerto Rican—face each other "across a crowded room"; again as then it is love at first sight. There is another echo across the centuries as both playwrights make use of hands and lips in this first encounter—to touch and kiss.

The action continues in parallel lines. Juliet's balcony becomes Maria's fire escape. Sondheim's lyric of "Tonight, Tonight" cannot touch Shakespeare's great love poetry of the balcony scene, but it nonetheless breathes ardor and adoration, which reach their culmination in the "wedding" scene of Act I Scene 7. Bernardo's knifing of Riff and the subsequent death of Bernardo at Tony's hand, which happens as the first act of *West Side Story* draws to a close, follows, of course, the pattern of killing and counter-killing of Mercutio by Tybalt, of Tybalt by Romeo. In the contemporary work, the tragic situation is complicated by the fact that Laurents makes Bernardo Maria's brother; and so much closer to her than was Tybalt to his cousin, Juliet.

The exile of Romeo results from public knowledge of his deed. Tony, not having been apprehended at the scene of the killing nor his guilt established by the police, becomes a fugitive. As a result of this altered circumstance the plot of *West Side Story* begins at this point to deviate from Shakespeare's drama. Doc, who is obviously intended as a counterpart of Friar Laurence, takes no comparably active role in the plotting. Tony plans an escape from town *with* Maria, not alone, meanwhile hiding in Doc's drugstore to await his rendezvous with her.

More significantly, the false report that the boy receives of the girl's death is carried by Anita through the gang as a willful act, not as an unfortuitous happenstance, such as befell Romeo because of the erroneous information Balthasar conveyed and the prevention of Friar John's delivery of the secret of Juliet's feigned death. Chance, which Shakespeare uses to bring about the final disaster, is eliminated by Laurents. Instead, the social prejudice, the mutual suspicion and hate that motivate the gang warfare become, in Act II Scene 4, the causes for Anita's lie about Maria's death and thus of the disaster that follows.

The greatest alterations in the plot occur in the brief final scene. Laurents eschews Shakespeare's scheme of the fake death of Juliet induced by potion to save her from marriage with Paris and to allow time for a reunion with Romeo. Consequently he faces the need to invent an ending that will be more believable to a modern audience. He does this by causing Tony to react to news of Chino's supposed murder of Maria by hurling himself into the arena crying, "Come and get me, too!" This gesture, intended as suicidal —for Tony no more wishes to live with Maria dead than Romeo wished to live without Juliet—accomplishes its end: Tony dies by a bullet from Chino's gun, a victim of the latter's revenge.

But the final moment is even more significant, for the curtain falls with Laurents' Paris and Juliet (Chino and Maria) still alive. Why this departure from the original tale? It has been suggested that avoidance of a general holocaust was out of a desire to make the ending more commercially palatable to Broadway audiences. This can be hardly valid, for a truly sentimental "soap-opera" denouement would somehow have saved both protagonists from death and reunited them in life.

To understand what this alteration in the story means, requires us to turn from purely plot considerations to look at character and at Laurents intent as opposed to Shakespeare's. The contemporary American playwright obviously feels that suicide is inconsistent with his heroine's character, that her death by her own hand would only diminish her stature. More significantly, however, her act of *not* killing herself or any of the gang members whom she threatens in the final scene, underlines the basic difference between this play and Shakespeare's: *West Side Story* is conceived as a social document, *Romeo and Juliet* as a *Liebestod*. Consequently, it becomes important to the contemporary play's message that a resolution of the gang warfare be effected, not as a postscript, so to speak, but by the hand of one of the play's protagonists.

When the poet W. H. Auden says of *Romeo and Juliet* that it "is not simply a tragedy of two individuals but the tragedy of a city. Everybody in the city is in one way or another involved in and responsible for what happens," he speaks more accurately of *West Side Story* than of Shakespeare's play. The feud of the Montagues and Capulets is never satisfactorily motivated; indeed, Shakespeare does not even attempt to do so, seeking to satisfy his audience simply by telling them that "Two households . . . from ancient grudge break to new mutiny." But the rivalry of the Sharks and the Jets is sociologically based on a familiar urban problem. Both the ancient Veronese houses were alike in privilege and station; their enmity was unreasonable, so far as we can judge. The cause of the West Side Manhattan gangs' rivalry is completely clear: it is between first-generation Americans whose security—social and economic—they feel to be jeopardized by the Puerto Ricans ("My old man says them Puerto Ricans is ruinin' free ennaprise," remarks Baby John), and the newcomers, fighting to establish themselves in an alien community. The tooth-and-nail defense of the former's tenuous priority is bound to force a tooth-and-nail reaction. That a London seventeenth-century Globe Theatre audience could have felt much concern for the municipal health of Verona or for the imaginary houses of Montague and Capulet is unlikely. That a contemporary American public, especially teen-agers themselves, could see in *West Side Story* a pressing problem to which some reference is made almost daily in their newspapers, is obvious. The modern play deals with a tragedy through which we are all living. "We all killed him!" cries Maria, as she stands beside her fallen lover, and we know she speaks truly.

It is as a social comment that *West Side Story* seems to make its greatest impact. What, then, one asks, is the likelihood of this play's outliving the solution of the social problem it deals with so eloquently—for an eventual solution, one is bound to believe, will come? Is it made of as enduring stuff as *Romeo and Juliet*? It is always dangerous, and perhaps meaningless, to hazard a guess about a candidacy for immortality: time alone will tell.

Despite Mr. Auden's assertion, *Romeo and Juliet* does live primarily as the tragedy of two individuals, of two young lovers who cared more for each other than for life itself. Nowadays, it is fashionable to say that people do not kill themselves for love; before doing so they would seek aid and comfort from their psychiatrists. While this may be true, it does not prevent us from being moved by the spectacle of persons who *have* died for love. Shakespeare makes us believe in his lovers, in their death, even in the improbabilities of chance that directs their lives. And his principal weapon is language.

What glorious verse falls from the lips of Shakespeare's boys and girls! True, there is a rollicking jazzy vigor in such songs of *West Side Story* as the one to Officer Krupke, but it pales alongside the pyrotechnical display of Mercutio's Queen Mab speech. There is tenderness in "Maria," but how relatively tongue-tied is the twentieth-century hero alongside the boy who cried, "He jests at scars that never felt a wound." "Hold my hand and we're half-way there," say Maria and Tony to each other, and the understatement touches us. But "Gallop apace, you fiery-footed steeds" and the lines that follow glow with a glory that never diminishes. The comparisons of language could be multiplied, and always, of course, Shakespeare is bound to win.

Without its great poetry *Romeo and Juliet* would not be a major tragedy. Possibly it is not, in any case; for as has frequently been remarked, Shakespeare's hero and heroine are a little too slender to carry the full weight of tragic grandeur. Their plight is more pathetic than tragic. If this is true of them, it is equally true of Tony and Maria: for them, too, pathos rather than tragedy. But there is tragedy implicit in the environmental situation of the contemporary couple, and this must not be overlooked or underestimated. Essentially, however, what we see is that all four young people strive to consummate the happiness at the threshold on which they stand and which they have tasted so briefly. All four are deprived of the opportunity to do so, the Renaissance couple by the caprice of fate, today's youngsters by the prejudice and hatred engendered around them. All four are courageous and lovable. All four arouse our compassion, even though they may not shake us with Aristotelian fear.

Poets and playwrights will continue to write of youthful lovers whom fate drives into and out of each other's lives. The spectacle will always trouble and move us, even as the two dramas in this volume do today.

—NORRIS HOUGHTON

ROMEO AND JULIET

BY WILLIAM SHAKESPEARE

DRAMATIS PERSONAE

CHORUS.
ESCALUS, PRINCE of Verona.
PARIS, a young Count, kinsman of the Prince.
MONTAGUE, } heads of two houses at variance
CAPULET, } with each other.
OLD MAN, of the Capulet family.
ROMEO, son of Montague.
MERCUTIO, kinsman of the Prince, and friend to Romeo.
BENVOLIO, nephew of Montague, and friend to Romeo.
TYBALT, nephew of Lady Capulet.
PETRUCHIO, a Capulet.
FRIAR LAURENCE, } Franciscans.
FRIAR JOHN, }
SAMPSON, }
GREGORY, }
ANTHONY, } servants to Capulet.
POTPAN, }
ABRAHAM, servant to Montague.
BALTHASAR, servant to Romeo.
PETER, servant to Juliet's nurse.
APOTHECARY.
SIMON CATLING, }
HUGH REBECK, } musicians.
JAMES SOUNDPOST, }
PAGE to PARIS; another PAGE; OFFICER.

LADY MONTAGUE, *wife of Montague.*
LADY CAPULET, *wife of Capulet.*
JULIET, *daughter of Capulet.*
NURSE *to Juliet.*
CITIZENS *of Verona;* GENTLEMEN *and* GENTLEWOMEN
    of both houses; MASKERS, TORCHBEARERS, GUARDS,
    WATCHMEN, SERVANTS, *and* ATTENDANTS.

SCENE: *Verona; Mantua.*

PROLOGUE

Enter Chorus

CHORUS

Two households both alike in dignity,
In fair Verona where we lay our scene,
From ancient grudge break to new mutiny,
Where civil blood makes civil hands unclean.
From forth the fatal loins of these two foes,   5
A pair of star-crossed lovers take their life;
Whose misadventured piteous overthrows
Doth with their death bury their parents' strife.
The fearful passage of their death-marked love,
And the continuance of their parents' rage,   10
Which, but their children's end, naught could remove,
Is now the two hours' traffic of our stage;
The which if you with patient ears attend,
What here shall miss, our toil shall strive to mend.
                                                        [*Exit.*]

Notes on this play begin on p. 225.

ACT I

SCENE ONE.

Verona. A public place. Enter Sampson and Gregory with swords and bucklers.

SAMPSON
Gregory, on my word we'll not carry coals.

GREGORY
No, for then we should be colliers.

SAMPSON
I mean, an we be in choler, we'll draw.

GREGORY
Ay, while you live, draw your neck out of collar. 5

SAMPSON
I strike quickly being moved.

GREGORY
But thou art not quickly moved to strike.

SAMPSON
A dog of the house of Montague moves me. 10

GREGORY
To move is to stir, and to be valiant is to stand.
Therefore if thou art moved thou run'st away.

SAMPSON
A dog of that house shall move me to stand. I
will take the wall of any man or maid of Montague's. 15

GREGORY
That shows thee a weak slave, for the weakest goes to
the wall.

SAMPSON
'Tis true, and therefore women being the weaker
vessels are ever thrust to the wall. Therefore I will 20

push Montague's men from the wall, and thrust his
maids to the wall.

GREGORY

The quarrel is between our masters and us their men.

SAMPSON

'Tis all one. I will show myself a tyrant. When I   25
have fought with the men, I will be cruel with the
maids—I will cut off their heads.

GREGORY

The heads of the maids?

SAMPSON

Ay the heads of the maids, or their maidenheads   30
—take it in what sense thou wilt.

GREGORY

They must take it in sense that feel it.

SAMPSON

Me they shall feel while I am able to stand, and 'tis
known I am a pretty piece of flesh.   35

GREGORY

'Tis well thou art not fish; if thou hadst, thou hadst
been Poor-John. Draw thy tool, here comes two of the
house of Montagues.

[*Enter Abraham and Balthasar.*]

SAMPSON

My naked weapon is out; quarrel, I will back thee.   40

GREGORY

How, turn thy back and run?

SAMPSON

Fear me not.

GREGORY

No marry, I fear thee!

SAMPSON

Let us take the law of our sides, let them begin.   45

GREGORY

I will frown as I pass by, and let them take it as they
list.

SAMPSON

Nay, as they dare, I will bite my thumb at them, which
is a disgrace to them if they bear it.   50

ABRAHAM

Do you bite your thumb at us sir?

SAMPSON

I do bite my thumb sir.

ABRAHAM

Do you bite your thumb at us sir?

SAMPSON [*aside to Gregory*]

Is the law of our side if I say ay?   55

GREGORY [*aside to Sampson*]

No.

SAMPSON

No sir, I do not bite my thumb at you sir, but I bite
my thumb sir.

GREGORY

Do you quarrel sir?

ABRAHAM

Quarrel sir? No sir.   60

SAMPSON

But if you do sir, I am for you; I serve as good a man
as you.

ABRAHAM

No better.

SAMPSON

Well sir.

[*Enter Benvolio.*]

GREGORY [*aside to Sampson*]

Say better; here comes one of my master's kinsmen.   65

SAMPSON

Yes, better sir.

ABRAHAM

You lie.

SAMPSON

Draw if you be men. Gregory, remember thy swash-
ing blow.   [*They fight*].   70

BENVOLIO

Part fools, [*Draws, and beats down their swords.*]
Put up your swords, you know not what you do.

[*Enter Tybalt.*]

TYBALT

What, art thou drawn among these heartless hinds?

Turn thee Benvolio, look upon thy death.
####### BENVOLIO
I do but keep the peace, put up thy sword,   75
Or manage it to part these men with me.
####### TYBALT
What, drawn and talk of peace? I hate the word,
As I hate hell, all Montagues, and thee.
Have at thee coward!   [*They fight.*]
        [*Enter Officer, and Citizens with clubs and
        partisans.*]
####### OFFICER
Clubs, bills, and partisans! Strike, beat them down.   80
####### CITIZENS
Down with the Capulets! Down with the Montagues!
        [*Enter Capulet in his gown, and Lady Capulet.*]
####### CAPULET
What noise is this? Give me my long sword, ho!
####### LADY CAPULET
A crutch, a crutch! Why call you for a sword?
                [*Enter Montague and Lady Montague.*]
####### CAPULET
My sword I say. Old Montague is come,
And flourishes his blade in spite of me.   85
####### MONTAGUE
Thou villain Capulet! Hold me not, let me go.
####### LADY MONTAGUE
Thou shalt not stir one foot to seek a foe.
                    [*Enter Prince Escalus, attended.*]
####### PRINCE
Rebellious subjects, enemies to peace,
Profaners of this neighbour-stained steel—
Will they not hear? What ho, you men, you beasts,   90
That quench the fire of your pernicious rage
With purple fountains issuing from your veins—
On pain of torture, from those bloody hands
Throw your mistempered weapons to the ground,
And hear the sentence of your moved Prince.   95
Three civil brawls bred of an airy word,
By thee old Capulet, and Montague,

Have thrice disturbed the quiet of our streets,
And made Verona's ancient citizens
Cast by their grave beseeming ornaments,   100
To wield old partisans, in hands as old,
Cankered with peace, to part your cankered hate.
If ever you disturb our streets again,
Your lives shall pay the forfeit of the peace.
For this time, all the rest depart away.   105
You Capulet shall go along with me;
And Montague, come you this afternoon,
To know our farther pleasure in this case,
To old Freetown, our common judgement-place
Once more, on pain of death, all men depart.   110

  [*Exeunt all but Montague, Lady Montague, and
  Benvolio.*]

  MONTAGUE

Who set this ancient quarrel new abroach?
Speak nephew, were you by when it began?

  BENVOLIO

Here were the servants of your adversary,
And yours, close fighting ere I did approach.
I drew to part them, in the instant came   115
The fiery Tybalt, with his sword prepared,
Which as he breathed defiance to my ears,
He swung about his head and cut the winds,
Who nothing hurt withal hissed him in scorn.
While we were interchanging thrusts and blows,   120
Came more and more, and fought on part and part,
Till the Prince came, who parted either part.

  LADY MONTAGUE

O where is Romeo? Saw you him to-day?
Right glad I am he was not at this fray.

  BENVOLIO

Madam, an hour before the worshipped sun   125
Peered forth the golden window of the east,
A troubled mind drave me to walk abroad,
Where underneath the grove of sycamore,
That westward rooteth from this city side,
So early walking did I see your son.   130
Towards him I made, but he was ware of me,

And stole into the covert of the wood.
I, measuring his affections by my own,
Which then most sought where most might not be
    found,
Being one too many by my weary self,
Pursued my humour, not pursuing his,   135
And gladly shunned who gladly fled from me.
      MONTAGUE
Many a morning hath he there been seen,
With tears augmenting the fresh morning's dew,
Adding to clouds more clouds with his deep sighs.
But all so soon as the all-cheering sun   140
Should in the farthest east begin to draw
The shady curtains from Aurora's bed,
Away from light steals home my heavy son,
And private in his chamber pens himself,
Shuts up his windows, locks fair daylight out,   145
And makes himself an artificial night.
Black and portentous must this humour prove,
Unless good counsel may the cause remove.
      BENVOLIO
My noble uncle, do you know the cause?
      MONTAGUE
I neither know it, nor can learn of him.   150
      BENVOLIO
Have you importuned him by any means?
      MONTAGUE
Both by my self and many other friends.
But he, his own affections' counsellor,
Is to himself—I will not say how true—
But to himself so secret and so close,   155
So far from sounding and discovery,
As is the bud bit with an envious worm,
Ere he can spread his sweet leaves to the air,
Or dedicate his beauty to the sun.
Could we but learn from whence his sorrows grow,   160
We would as willingly give cure as know.
                   [*Enter Romeo.*]
      BENVOLIO
See where he comes, so please you step aside.

I'll know his grievance or be much denied.

MONTAGUE

I would thou wert so happy by thy stay
To hear true shrift. Come madam, let's away.   165

[Exeunt Montague and Lady Montague.]

BENVOLIO

Good morrow cousin.

ROMEO

Is the day so young?

BENVOLIO

But new struck nine.

ROMEO

Ay me, sad hours seem long.

Was that my father that went hence so fast?

BENVOLIO

It was. What sadness lengthens Romeo's hours?

ROMEO

Not having that which having makes them short.   170

BENVOLIO

In love?

ROMEO

Out—

BENVOLIO

Of love?

ROMEO

Out of her favour where I am in love.

BENVOLIO

Alas that love, so gentle in his view,   175
Should be so tyrannous and rough in proof!

ROMEO

Alas that love, whose view is muffled still,
Should without eyes see pathways to his will.
Where shall we dine? O me, what fray was here?
Yet tell me not, for I have heard it all.   180
Here's much to do with hate, but more with love.
Why then, o brawling love, a loving hate,
O any thing of nothing first create!
O heavy lightness, serious vanity,
Misshapen chaos of well-seeming forms,   185
Feather of lead, bright smoke, cold fire, sick health,

Still-waking sleep, that is not what it is!
This love feel I, that feel no love in this.
Dost thou not laugh?
BENVOLIO
                              No coz, I rather weep.
ROMEO
Good heart, at what?
BENVOLIO
                              At thy good heart's oppression.   190
ROMEO
Why such is love's transgression.
Griefs of mine own lie heavy in my breast,
Which thou wilt propagate to have it pressed
With more of thine; this love that thou hast shown,
Doth add more grief, to too much of mine own.   195
Love is a smoke raised with the fume of sighs;
Being purged, a fire sparkling in lovers' eyes;
Being vexed, a sea nourished with lovers' tears.
What is it else? A madness most discreet,
A choking gall, and a preserving sweet.   200
Farewell my coz.
BENVOLIO
                              Soft, I will go along.
And if you leave me so, you do me wrong.
ROMEO
Tut I have lost myself; I am not here.
This is not Romeo, he's some other where.
BENVOLIO
Tell me in sadness, who is that you love.   205
ROMEO
What, shall I groan and tell thee?
BENVOLIO
                              Groan? Why no
But sadly tell me who.
ROMEO
Bid a sick man in sadness make his will!
Ah word ill urged to one that is so ill.
In sadness cousin, I do love a woman.   210
BENVOLIO
I aimed so near, when I supposed you loved.

ROMEO

A right good mark-man. And she's fair I love.

BENVOLIO

A right fair mark, fair coz, is soonest hit.

ROMEO

Well in that hit you miss, she'll not be hit
With Cupid's arrow. She hath Dian's wit,   215
And in strong proof of chastity well armed,
From love's weak childish bow she lives uncharmed.
She will not stay the siege of loving terms,
Nor bide th' encounter of assailing eyes,
Nor ope her lap to saint-seducing gold.   220
O she is rich in beauty, only poor,
That when she dies with beauty dies her store.

BENVOLIO

Then she hath sworn that she will still live chaste?

ROMEO

She hath, and in that sparing makes huge waste.
For beauty starved with her severity   225
Cuts beauty off from all posterity.
She is too fair, too wise; wisely too fair,
To merit bliss by making me despair.
She hath forsworn to love, and in that vow
Do I live dead that live to tell it now.   230

BENVOLIO

Be ruled by me, forget to think of her.

ROMEO

O teach me how I should forget to think.

BENVOLIO

By giving liberty unto thine eyes.
Examine other beauties.

ROMEO

                        'Tis the way
To call hers, exquisite, in question more.   235
These happy masks that kiss fair ladies' brows,
Being black, put us in mind they hide the fair.
He that is strucken blind cannot forget
The precious treasure of his eyesight lost.
Show me a mistress that is passing fair,   240
What doth her beauty serve, but as a note

Where I may read who passed that passing fair?
Farewell, thou canst not teach me to forget.
                    BENVOLIO
I'll pay that doctrine, or else die in debt. [*Exeunt.*]

SCENE TWO.

*The same. Enter Capulet,
Paris, and Servant.*

                    CAPULET
But Montague is bound as well as I,
In penalty alike; and 'tis not hard, I think,
For men so old as we to keep the peace.
                    PARIS
Of honourable reckoning are you both,
And pity 'tis you lived at odds so long.
But now my lord, what say you to my suit?   5
                    CAPULET
But saying o'er what I have said before.
My child is yet a stranger in the world,
She hath not seen the change of fourteen years.
Let two more summers wither in their pride   10
Ere we may think her ripe to be a bride.
                    PARIS
Younger than she are happy mothers made.
                    CAPULET
And too soon marred are those so early made.
Earth hath swallowed all my hopes but she:
She is the hopeful lady of my earth.   15
But woo her gentle Paris, get her heart,
My will to her consent is but a part.
An she agree, within her scope of choice
Lies my consent and fair according voice.
This night I hold an old accustomed feast,   20

Whereto I have invited many a guest,
Such as I love; and you among the store,
One more, most welcome, makes my number more.
At my poor house look to behold this night
Earth-treading stars that make dark heaven light.   25
Such comfort as do lusty young men feel,
When well-apparelled April on the heel
Of limping Winter treads, even such delight
Among fresh female buds shall you this night
Inherit at my house; hear all, all see,   30
And like her most whose merit most shall be:
Which on more view of many, mine being one
May stand in number, though in reckoning none.
Come go with me. [*To Servant, giving him a paper.*]
    Go sirrah, trudge about
Through fair Verona, find those persons out   35
Whose names are written there, and to them say,
My house and welcome on their pleasure stay.
                                    [*Exeunt Capulet and Paris.*]

            SERVANT
Find them out whose names are written here! It
is written that the shoemaker should meddle with his
yard, and the tailor with his last, the fisher with his   40
pencil, and the painter with his nets. But I am
sent to find those persons whose names are here writ,
and can never find what names the writing person
hath here writ. I must to the learned, in good
time.   45
                            [*Enter Benvolio and Romeo.*]

        BENVOLIO
Tut man, one fire burns out another's burning,
One pain is lessened by another's anguish;
Turn giddy, and be holp by backward turning;
One desperate grief cures with another's languish.
Take thou some new infection to thy eye,   50
And the rank poison of the old will die.

        ROMEO
Your plantain leaf is excellent for that.

        BENVOLIO
For what I pray thee?

ROMEO
                    For your broken shin.
BENVOLIO
Why Romeo, art thou mad?
ROMEO
Not mad, but bound more than a madman is;   55
Shut up in prison, kept without my food,
Whipped and tormented, and——God-den good fellow.
SERVANT
God gi' god-den, I pray sir can you read?
ROMEO
Ay, mine own fortune in my misery.   60
SERVANT
Perhaps you have learned it without book. But I pray
can you read any thing you see?
ROMEO
Ay, if I know the letters and the language.
SERVANT
Ye say honestly, rest you merry.   65
ROMEO
Stay fellow, I can read.   [*Reads the paper:*]
    Seigneur Martino, and his wife and daughters;
County Anselme and his beauteous sisters; the lady
widow of Vitruvio, Seigneur Placentio, and his lovely
nieces; Mercutio and his brother Valentine; mine   70
uncle Capulet, his wife and daughters; my fair niece
Rosaline, Livia, Seigneur Valentio, and his cousin
Tybalt; Lucio and the lively Helena.
                        [*Gives back the paper.*]
A fair assembly: whither should they come?   75
SERVANT
Up.
ROMEO
Whither? To supper?
SERVANT
To our house.
ROMEO
Whose house?
SERVANT
My master's.   80

ROMEO

Indeed I should have asked you that before.

SERVANT

Now I'll tell you without asking. My master is the
great rich Capulet, and if you be not of the house of
Montagues, I pray come and crush a cup of wine.   85
Rest you merry.   [*Exit.*]

BENVOLIO

At this same ancient feast of Capulet's
Sups the fair Rosaline whom thou so loves,
With all the admired beauties of Verona.
Go thither, and with unattainted eye,   90
Compare her face with some that I shall show,
And I will make thee think thy swan a crow.

ROMEO

When the devout religion of mine eye
Maintains such falsehood, then turn tears to fires;
And these who often drowned could never die,   95
Transparent heretics, be burnt for liars.
One fairer than my love—the all-seeing sun
Ne'er saw her match, since first the world begun.

BENVOLIO

Tut you saw her fair, none else being by,
Herself poised with herself in either eye.   100
But in that crystal scales let there be weighed
Your lady's love against some other maid
That I will show you shining at this feast,
And she shall scant show well that now shows best.

ROMEO

I'll go along, no such sight to be shown,   105
But to rejoice in splendour of mine own.

[*Exeunt.*]

SCENE THREE.

Verona. Capulet's house.
Enter Lady Capulet and Nurse.

LADY CAPULET
Nurse, where's my daughter? Call her forth to me.
    NURSE
Now by my maidenhead—at twelve year old—I bade
her come. What lamb! What lady-bird! God forbid!
Where's this girl? What, Juliet!

                         [Enter Juliet.]

    JULIET
How now? Who calls?
    NURSE
Your mother.
    JULIET
Madam, I am here, what is your will?   5
    LADY CAPULET
This is the matter—nurse, give leave awhile,
We must talk in secret. Nurse, come back again,
I have remembered me. Thou's hear our counsel.
Thou knowest my daughter's of a pretty age.   10
    NURSE
Faith I can tell her age unto an hour.
    LADY CAPULET
She's not fourteen.
    NURSE
I'll lay fourteen of my teeth, and yet to my teen be
it spoken, I have but four, she's not fourteen. How
long is it now to Lammas-tide?
    LADY CAPULET
A fortnight and odd days.   15
    NURSE
Even or odd, of all days in the year,
Come Lammas Eve at night shall she be fourteen.
Susan and she—God rest all Christian souls—

Were of an age. Well, Susan is with God,
She was too good for me. But as I said, 20
On Lammas Eve at night shall she be fourteen;
That shall she marry, I remember it well.
'Tis since the earthquake now eleven years,
And she was weaned—I never shall forget it—
Of all the days of the year, upon that day. 25
For I had then laid wormwood to my dug,
Sitting in the sun under the dove-house wall.
My lord and you were then at Mantua—
Nay I do bear a brain—but as I said,
When it did taste the wormwood on the nipple 30
Of my dug, and felt it bitter, pretty fool,
To see it tetchy and fall out with the dug!
Shake, quoth the dove-house; 'twas no need I trow
To bid me trudge.
And since that time it is eleven years, 35
For then she could stand high-lone; nay by th' rood,
She could have run and waddled all about;
For even the day before, she broke her brow,
And then my husband—God be with his soul,
'A was a merry man—took up the child. 40
Yea, quoth he, dost thou fall upon thy face?
Thou wilt fall backward when thou hast more wit,
Wilt thou not Jule? And by my holidame,
The pretty wretch left crying, and said ay.
To see now how a jest shall come about! 45
I warrant, an I should live a thousand years,
I never should forget it. Wilt thou not Jule, quoth he,
And pretty fool it stinted, and said ay.
        LADY CAPULET
Enough of this, I pray thee hold thy peace.
        NURSE
Yes madam, yet I cannot choose but laugh, 50
To think it should leave crying, and say ay.
And yet I warrant it had upon it brow
A bump as big as a young cockerel's stone.
A perilous knock, and it cried bitterly.
Yea, quoth my husband, fall'st upon thy face? 55
Thou wilt fall backward when thou comest to age;

Wilt thou not Jule? It stinted, and said ay.
> JULIET

And stint thou too, I pray thee nurse, say I.
> NURSE

Peace, I have done. God mark thee to his grace;
Thou wast the prettiest babe that e'er I nursed;   60
An I might live to see thee married once,
I have my wish.
> LADY CAPULET

Marry, that marry is the very theme
I came to talk of. Tell me daughter Juliet,
How stands your dispositions to be married?   65
> JULIET

It is an honour that I dream not of.
> NURSE

An honour? Were not I thine only nurse,
I would say thou hadst sucked wisdom from thy teat.
> LADY CAPULET

Well, think of marriage now. Younger than you,
Here in Verona, ladies of esteem,   70
Are made already mothers. By my count,
I was your mother much upon these years
That you are now a maid. Thus then in brief—
The valiant Paris seeks you for his love.
> NURSE

A man, young lady; lady, such a man   75
As all the world—why he's a man of wax.
> LADY CAPULET

Verona's summer hath not such a flower.
> NURSE

Nay he's a flower, in faith a very flower.
> LADY CAPULET

What say you, can you love the gentleman?
This night you shall behold him at our feast,   80
Read o'er the volume of young Paris' face,
And find delight writ there with beauty's pen;
Examine every married lineament,
And see how one another lends content;
And what obscured in this fair volume lies   85
Find written in the margent of his eyes.

This precious book of love, this unbound lover,
To beautify him only lacks a cover.
The fish lives in the sea, and 'tis much pride
For fair without the fair within to hide.   90
That book in many's eyes doth share the glory,
That in gold clasps locks in the golden story;
So shall you share all that he doth possess,
By having him, making yourself no less.

NURSE   95
No less, nay bigger; women grow by men.

LADY CAPULET
Speak briefly, can you like of Paris' love?

JULIET
I'll look to like, if looking liking move.
But no more deep will I endart mine eye
Than your consent gives strength to make it fly.
                                   [Enter Servant.]

SERVANT
Madam the guests are come, supper served up, you   100
called, my young lady asked for, the nurse cursed in
the pantry, and every thing in extremity. I must hence
to wait; I beseech you follow straight.

LADY CAPULET
We follow thee. [Exit Servant.] Juliet, the County
stays.   105

NURSE
Go girl, seek happy nights to happy days.
                                   [Exeunt.]

SCENE FOUR.

Verona. A street. Enter Romeo, Mercutio,
Benvolio, with other Maskers,
and Torchbearers.

ROMEO
What, shall this speech be spoke for our excuse?
Or shall we on without apology?

BENVOLIO

The date is out of such prolixity.
We'll have no Cupid hoodwinked with a scarf,
Bearing a Tartar's painted bow of lath,   5
Scaring the ladies like a crow-keeper;
Nor no without-book prologue, faintly spoke
After the prompter, for our entrance.
But let them measure us by what they will,
We'll measure them a measure, and be gone.   10

ROMEO

Give me a torch, I am not for this ambling;
Being but heavy, I will bear the light.

MERCUTIO

Nay gentle Romeo, we must have you dance.

ROMEO

Not I, believe me, you have dancing shoes
With nimble soles, I have a soul of lead   15
So stakes me to the ground I cannot move.

MERCUTIO

You are a lover, borrow Cupid's wings,
And soar with them above a common bound.

ROMEO

I am too sore enpierced with his shaft,
To soar with his light feathers; and so bound,   20
I cannot bound a pitch above dull woe.
Under love's heavy burden do I sink.

MERCUTIO

And to sink in it should you burden love;
Too great oppression for a tender thing.

ROMEO

Is love a tender thing? It is too rough,   25
Too rude, too boisterous, and it pricks like thorn.

MERCUTIO

If love be rough with you, be rough with love.
Prick love for pricking, and you beat love down.
Give me a case to put my visage in.

[Puts on a mask.]

A visor for a visor. What care I   30
What curious eye doth quote deformities?
Here are the beetle brows shall blush for me.

BENVOLIO
Come knock and enter, and no sooner in,
But every man betake him to his legs.
ROMEO
A torch for me; let wantons light of heart   35
Tickle the senseless rushes with their heels.
For I am proverbed with a grandsire phrase—
I'll be a candle-holder and look on—
The game was ne'er so fair, and I am done.
MERCUTIO
Tut, dun's the mouse, the constable's own word.   40
If thou are Dun, we'll draw thee from the mire
Of this sir-reverence love, wherein thou stickest
Up to the ears. Come, we burn daylight, ho!
ROMEO
Nay that's not so.
MERCUTIO
                I mean sir, in delay
We waste our lights in vain, like lamps by day.   45
Take our good meaning, for our judgment sits
Five times in that, ere once in our five wits.
ROMEO
And we mean well in going to this mask;
But 'tis no wit to go.
MERCUTIO
                Why, may one ask?
ROMEO
I dreamt a dream to-night.
MERCUTIO
                        And so did I.   50
ROMEO
Well, what was yours?
MERCUTIO
                    That dreamers often lie.
ROMEO
In bed asleep while they do dream things true.
MERCUTIO
O then I see Queen Mab hath been with you.
She is the fairies' midwife, and she comes
In shape no bigger than an agate stone   55

On the forefinger of an alderman,
Drawn with a team of little atomies
Over men's noses as they lie asleep.
Her wagon-spokes made of long spinners' legs;
The cover, of the wings of grasshoppers; 60
Her traces, of the smallest spider web;
Her collars, of the moonshine's watery beams;
Her whip of cricket's bone; the lash of film;
Her wagoner, a small gray-coated gnat,
Not half so big as a round little worm, 65
Pricked from the lazy finger of a maid.
Her chariot is an empty hazel-nut,
Made by the joiner squirrel or old grub,
Time out a mind the fairies' coachmakers.
And in this state she gallops night by night 70
Through lovers' brains, and then they dream of love;
O'er courtiers' knees, that dream on curtsies straight;
O'er lawyers' fingers, who straight dream on fees;
O'er ladies' lips, who straight on kisses dream,
Which oft the angry Mab with blisters plagues, 75
Because their breaths with sweetmeats tainted are.
Sometime she gallops o'er a courtier's nose,
And then dreams he of smelling out a suit;
And sometime comes she with a tithe-pig's tail,
Tickling a parson's nose as 'a lies asleep, 80
Then he dreams of another benefice.
Sometime she driveth o'er a soldier's neck,
And then dreams he of cutting foreign throats,
Of breaches, ambuscadoes, Spanish blades,
Of healths five fathom deep; and then anon 85
Drums in his ear, at which he starts and wakes;
And being thus frighted, swears a prayer or two,
And sleeps again. This is that very Mab
That plats the manes of horses in the night,
And bakes the elf-locks in foul sluttish hairs. 90
Which once untangled, much misfortune bodes.
This is the hag, when maids lie on their backs,
That presses them and learns them first to bear,
Making them women of good carriage.
This is she—

ROMEO

          Peace, peace, Mercutio, peace.   95
Thou talk'st of nothing.

MERCUTIO

                True, I talk of dreams;
Which are the children of an idle brain,
Begot of nothing but vain fantasy;
Which is as thin of substance as the air,
And more inconstant than the wind who wooes   100
Even now the frozen bosom of the north,
And being angered puffs away from thence,
Turning his side to the dew-dropping south.

BENVOLIO

This wind you talk of blows us from ourselves.
Supper is done, and we shall come too late.   105

ROMEO

I fear, too early; for my mind misgives
Some consequence, yet hanging in the stars,
Shall bitterly begin his fearful date
With this night's revels, and expire the term
Of a despised life closed in my breast,   110
By some vile forfeit of untimely death.
But he that hath the steerage of my course
Direct my sail. On lusty gentlemen.

BENVOLIO

Strike drum.

      [They march about the stage, and exeunt.]

SCENE FIVE.

*Verona. A hall in Capulet's house.
Enter Musicians, and two Servants
with napkins.*

FIRST SERVANT

Where's Potpan, that he helps not to take away?
He shift a trencher? He scrape a trencher?

SECOND SERVANT

When good manners shall lie all in one or two men's
hands, and they unwashed too, 'tis a foul thing.   5

FIRST SERVANT

Away with the joint-stools, remove the court-cupboard,
look to the plate. Good thou, save me a piece of
marchpane, and as thou loves me, let the porter let in
Susan Grindstone and Nell.   10

[Exit Second Servant.]

Anthony and Potpan!

[Enter Anthony and Potpan.]

ANTHONY

Ay boy, ready.

FIRST SERVANT

You are looked for, and called for, asked for, and
sought for in the great chamber.

POTPAN

We cannot be here and there too. Cheerly boys, be   15
brisk awhile, and the longer liver take all.

[They retire.]

[Enter the Maskers at one door, and at the
other Capulet, Lady Capulet, Juliet, Nurse,
Tybalt, and others of the house and Guests,
meeting.]

CAPULET

Welcome gentlemen. Ladies that have their toes
Unplagued with corns will walk a bout with you.
Ah ha, my mistresses, which of you all   20
Will now deny to dance? She that makes dainty,
She I'll swear hath corns. Am I come near ye now?
Welcome gentlemen. I have seen the day
That I have worn a visor and could tell
A whispering tale in a fair lady's ear,   25
Such as would please. 'Tis gone, 'tis gone, 'tis gone.
You are welcome, gentlemen. Come, musicians play.
A hall, a hall, give room, and foot it girls.

[Music plays, and they dance.]

More light you knaves, and turn the tables up;
And quench the fire, the room is grown too hot.   30
Ah sirrah, this unlooked for sport comes well.
Nay sit, nay sit, good cousin Capulet,
For you and I are past our dancing days.
How long is't now since last yourself and I
Were in a mask?

SECOND CAPULET
            By'r lady, thirty years.   35

CAPULET
What man, 'tis not so much, 'tis not so much;
'Tis since the nuptial of Lucentio,
Come Pentecost as quickly as it will,
Some five and twenty years, and then we masked.

SECOND CAPULET
'Tis more, 'tis more, his son is elder sir;   40
His son is thirty.

CAPULET
            Will you tell me that?
His son was but a ward two years ago.

ROMEO [to a Servant]
What lady's that which doth enrich the hand
Of yonder knight?

SERVANT
I know not sir.   45

ROMEO
O she doth teach the torches to burn bright.
It seems she hangs upon the cheek of night
As a rich jewel in an Ethiop's ear;
Beauty too rich for use, for earth too dear.
So shows a snowy dove trooping with crows,   50
As yonder lady o'er her fellows shows.
The measure done, I'll watch her place of stand,
And touching hers make blessed my rude hand.
Did my heart love till now? Forswear it sight,
For I ne'er saw true beauty till this night.   55

TYBALT
This by his voice should be a Montague.
Fetch me my rapier, boy. What dares the slave
Come hither covered with an antic face,

To fleer and scorn at our solemnity?
Now by the stock and honour of my kin,   60
To strike him dead I hold it not a sin.

CAPULET

Why how now kinsman, wherefore storm you so?

TYBALT

Uncle, this is a Montague, our foe;
A villain that is hither come in spite,
To scorn at our solemnity this night.   65

CAPULET

Young Romeo is it?

TYBALT

             'Tis he, that villain Romeo.

CAPULET

Content thee gentle coz, let him alone.
'A bears him like a portly gentleman;
And to say truth, Verona brags of him
To be a virtuous and well governed youth.   70
I would not for the wealth of all this town
Here in my house do him disparagement.
Therefore be patient, take no note of him;
It is my will, the which if thou respect,
Show a fair presence, and put off these frowns,   75
An ill-beseeming semblance for a feast.

TYBALT

It fits when such a villain is a guest.
I'll not endure him.

CAPULET

           He shall be endured.
What goodman boy, I say he shall; go to,
Am I the master here or you? Go to.   80
You'll not endure him? God shall mend my soul,
You'll make a mutiny among my guests?
You will set cock-a-hoop, you'll be the man?

TYBALT

Why uncle, 'tis a shame—

CAPULET

           Go to, go to,
You are a saucy boy. Is't so indeed?   85
This trick may chance to scathe you, I know what.

You must contrary me? Marry 'tis time.
Well said my hearts! You are a princox, go;
Be quiet, or—more light, more light! For shame!
I'll make you quiet. What, cheerly my hearts!   90

TYBALT
Patience perforce with wilful choler meeting
Makes my flesh tremble in their different greeting.
I will withdraw, but this intrusion shall,
Now seeming sweet, convert to bitt'rest gall.

                                                        [*Exit.*]

ROMEO [*to Juliet*]
If I profane with my unworthiest hand   95
This holy shrine, the gentle sin is this,
My lips two blushing pilgrims ready stand
To smooth that rough touch with a tender kiss.

JULIET
Good pilgrim, you do wrong your hand too much,
Which mannerly devotion shows in this;   100
For saints have hands that pilgrims' hands do touch,
And palm to palm is holy palmers' kiss.

ROMEO
Have not saints lips, and holy palmers too?

JULIET
Ay pilgrim, lips that they must use in prayer.

ROMEO
O then dear saint, let lips do what hands do.   105
They pray; grant thou, lest faith turn to despair.

JULIET
Saints do not move, though grant for prayers' sake.

ROMEO
Then move not while my prayer's effect I take.
Thus from my lips, by thine, my sin is purged.

JULIET
Then have my lips the sin that they have took.   110

ROMEO
Sin from my lips? O trespass sweetly urged.
Give me my sin again.

JULIET
                    You kiss by th' book.

NURSE

Madam, your mother craves a word with you.

ROMEO

What is her mother?

NURSE

              Marry bachelor,

Her mother is the lady of the house,   115

And a good lady, and a wise and virtuous.

I nursed her daughter that you talked withal.

I tell you, he that can lay hold of her

Shall have the chinks.

ROMEO

              Is she a Capulet?

O dear account, my life is my foe's debt.   120

BENVOLIO

Away, be gone; the sport is at the best.

ROMEO

Ay, so I fear, the more is my unrest.

CAPULET

Nay gentlemen, prepare not to be gone;

We have a trifling foolish banquet towards.

Is it e'en so? Why then I thank you all.   125

I thank you, honest gentlemen; good night.

More torches here! Come on, then, let's to bed.

[*To second Capulet.*] Ah sirrah, by my fay, it waxes
late.

I'll to my rest. [*Exeunt all but Juliet and Nurse.*]

JULIET

Come hither nurse. What is yond gentleman?   130

NURSE

The son and heir of old Tiberio.

JULIET

What's he that now is going out of door?

NURSE

Marry that I think be young Petruchio.

JULIET

What's he that follows here that would not dance?

NURSE

I know not.   135

JULIET

Go ask his name—if he be married,
My grave is like to be my wedding-bed.

NURSE

His name is Romeo, and a Montague;
The only son of your great enemy.

JULIET

My only love sprung from my only hate,   140
Too early seen unknown, and known too late!
Prodigious birth of love it is to me,
That I must love a loathed enemy.

NURSE

What's this, what's this?

JULIET

A rhyme I learned even now
Of one I danced withal.   [*A call within*, Juliet.]

NURSE

Anon, anon!   145
Come let's away, the strangers all are gone.

[*Exeunt.*]

ACT II

PROLOGUE

Enter Chorus.

Now old desire doth in his death-bed lie,
And young affection gapes to be his heir;
That fair for which love groaned for and would die,
With tender Juliet matched, is now not fair.
Now Romeo is beloved, and loves again,   5
Alike bewitched by the charm of looks;
But to his foe supposed he must complain,
And she steal love's sweet bait from fearful hooks.
Being held a foe, he may not have access
To breathe such vows as lovers use to swear;   10
And she as much in love, her means much less
To meet her new beloved any where.
But passion lends them power, time means, to meet,
Temp'ring extremities with extreme sweet.   [*Exit.*]

SCENE ONE.

*Verona. Capulet's walled orchard and a
lane by it. Enter Romeo in the lane.*

ROMEO
Can I go forward when my heart is here?

Turn back, dull earth, and find thy centre out.
>[*Climbs over the orchard wall. Enter Benvolio*
>*and Mercutio in the lane.*]

BENVOLIO

Romeo! My cousin Romeo! Romeo!

MERCUTIO

                              He is wise,
And on my life hath stolen him home to bed.

BENVOLIO

He ran this way and leaped this orchard wall.   5
Call, good Mercutio.

MERCUTIO

                 Nay I'll conjure too.
Romeo! Humours! Madman! Passion! Lover!
Appear thou in the likeness of a sigh,
Speak but one rhyme and I am satisfied;
Cry but, ay me, pronounce but love and dove;   10
Speak to my gossip Venus one fair word,
One nickname for her purblind son and heir,
Young Abraham Cupid, he that shot so true,
When King Cophetua loved the beggar-maid.
He heareth not, he stirreth not, he moveth not;   15
The ape is dead, and I must conjure him.
I conjure thee by Rosaline's bright eyes,
By her high forehead, and her scarlet lip,
By her fine foot, straight leg, and quivering thigh,
And the demesnes that there adjacent lie,   20
That in thy likeness thou appear to us.

BENVOLIO

An if he hear thee thou wilt anger him.

MERCUTIO

This cannot anger him; 'twould anger him
To raise a spirit in his mistress' circle
Of some strange nature, letting it there stand   25
Till she had laid it and conjured it down;
That were some spite. My invocation
Is fair and honest; in his mistress' name
I conjure only but to raise up him.

BENVOLIO

Come, he hath hid himself among these trees   30

To be consorted with the humorous night.
Blind is his love, and best befits the dark.
> MERCUTIO
If love be blind, love cannot hit the mark.
Now will he sit under a medlar tree,
And wish his mistress were that kind of fruit   35
As maids call medlars, when they laugh alone.
O Romeo that she were, o that she were
An open et cetera, thou a poperin pear.
Romeo good night, I'll to my truckle bed;
This field-bed is too cold for me to sleep.   40
Come, shall we go?
> BENVOLIO
>   Go then, for 'tis in vain
To seek him here that means not to be found.
>   *[Exeunt Benvolio and Mercutio.]*

SCENE TWO.

The same.

> ROMEO *[comes forward]*
He jests at scars that never felt a wound.
>   *[Enter Juliet above.]*
But soft, what light through yonder window breaks?
It is the East, and Juliet is the sun.
Arise fair sun and kill the envious moon,
Who is already sick and pale with grief,   5
That thou her maid art far more fair than she.
Be not her maid since she is envious,
Her vestal livery is but sick and green,
And none but fools do wear it; cast it off.
It is my lady, o it is my love.   10
O that she knew she were.
She speaks, yet she says nothing; what of that?

Her eye discourses, I will answer it.
I am too bold, 'tis not to me she speaks.
Two of the fairest stars in all the heaven,   15
Having some business, do entreat her eyes
To twinkle in their spheres till they return.
What if her eyes were there, they in her head?
The brightness of her cheek would shame those stars,
As daylight doth a lamp; her eyes in heaven   20
Would through the airy region stream so bright,
That birds would sing, and think it were not night.
See how she leans her cheek upon her hand.
O that I were a glove upon that hand,
That I might touch that cheek.

    JULIET

                  Ay me!

    ROMEO

                        She speaks.   25
O speak again bright angel, for thou art
As glorious to this night being o'er my head,
As is a winged messenger of heaven
Unto the white-upturned wond'ring eyes
Of mortals that fall back to gaze on him,   30
When he bestrides the lazy pacing clouds,
And sails upon the bosom of the air.

    JULIET

O Romeo, Romeo, wherefore art thou Romeo?
Deny thy father, and refuse thy name.
Or if thou wilt not, be but sworn my love,   35
And I'll no longer be a Capulet.

    ROMEO

Shall I hear more, or shall I speak at this?

    JULIET

'Tis but thy name that is my enemy.
Thou art thyself, though not a Montague.
What's Montague? It is nor hand nor foot,   40
Nor arm nor face, nor any other part
Belonging to a man. O be some other name.
What's in a name? That which we call a rose
By any other word would smell as sweet;
So Romeo would, were he not Romeo called,   45

Retain that dear perfection which he owes
Without that title. Romeo doff thy name,
And for thy name which is no part of thee,
Take all myself.

ROMEO

    I take thee at thy word.
Call me but love, and I'll be new baptized; 50
Henceforth I never will be Romeo.

JULIET

What man art thou, that thus bescreened in night
So stumblest on my counsel?

ROMEO

     By a name
I know not how to tell thee who I am.
My name, dear saint, is hateful to myself, 55
Because it is an enemy to thee.
Had I it written, I would tear the word.

JULIET

My ears have not yet drunk a hundred words
Of thy tongue's uttering, yet I know the sound.
Art thou not Romeo, and a Montague? 60

ROMEO

Neither, fair maid, if either thee dislike.

JULIET

How cam'st thou hither, tell me, and wherefore?
The orchard walls are high and hard to climb,
And the place death, considering who thou art,
If any of my kinsmen find thee here. 65

ROMEO

With love's light wings did I o'er-perch these walls,
For stony limits cannot hold love out,
And what love can do, that dares love attempt.
Therefore thy kinsmen are no stop to me.

JULIET

If they do see thee, they will murder thee. 70

ROMEO

Alack there lies more peril in thine eye
Than twenty of their swords; look thou but sweet,
And I am proof against their enmity.

JULIET

I would not for the world they saw thee here.

ROMEO

I have night's cloak to hide me from their eyes.   75
And but thou love me, let them find me here.
My life were better ended by their hate,
Than death prorogued, wanting of thy love.

JULIET

By whose direction found'st thou out this place?

ROMEO

By love that first did prompt me to enquire;   80
He lent me counsel, and I lent him eyes.
I am no pilot, yet wert thou as far
As that vast shore washed with the farthest sea,
I should adventure for such merchandise.

JULIET

Thou knowest the mask of night is on my face,   85
Else would a maiden blush bepaint my cheek,
For that which thou hast heard me speak tonight.
Fain would I dwell on form, fain, fain, deny
What I have spoke; but farewell compliment.
Dost thou love me? I know thou wilt say ay,   90
And I will take thy word; yet if thou swear'st,
Thou mayst prove false; at lovers' perjuries
They say Jove laughs. O gentle Romeo,
If thou dost love, pronounce it faithfully.
Or if thou thinkest I am too quickly won,   95
I'll frown and be perverse, and say thee nay,
So thou wilt woo; but else not for the world.
In truth fair Montague I am too fond;
And therefore thou mayst think my haviour light.
But trust me gentleman, I'll prove more true   100
Than those that have more cunning to be strange.
I should have been more strange, I must confess,
But that thou overheard'st, ere I was ware,
My true love's passion; therefore pardon me,
And not impute this yielding to light love,   105
Which the dark night hath so discovered.

ROMEO

Lady, by yonder blessed moon I vow,

That tips with silver all these fruit tree tops—
    J U L I E T
O swear not by the moon, th' inconstant moon,
That monthly changes in her circled orb,   110
Lest that thy love prove likewise variable.
    R O M E O
What shall I swear by?
    J U L I E T
                  Do not swear at all.
Or if thou wilt, swear by thy gracious self,
Which is the god of my idolatry,
And I'll believe thee.
    R O M E O
                If my heart's dear love—   115
    J U L I E T
Well do not swear. Although I joy in thee,
I have no joy of this contract to-night,
It is too rash, too unadvised, too sudden,
Too like the lightning, which doth cease to be
Ere one can say, it lightens. Sweet, good night.   120
This bud of love by summer's ripening breath
May prove a beauteous flower when next we meet.
Good night, good night. As sweet repose and rest
Come to thy heart as that within my breast.
    R O M E O
O wilt thou leave me so unsatisfied?   125
    J U L I E T
What satisfaction canst thou have to-night?
    R O M E O
Th' exchange of thy love's faithful vow for mine.
    J U L I E T
I gave thee mine before thou didst request it.
And yet I would it were to give again.
    R O M E O
Wouldst thou withdraw it? For what purpose, love?   130
    J U L I E T
But to be frank and give it thee again;
And yet I wish but for the thing I have.
My bounty is as boundless as the sea,
My love as deep; the more I give to thee

The more I have, for both are infinite.   135

                        [Nurse calls within.]

I hear some noise within; dear love adieu.
Anon good nurse! Sweet Montague, be true.
Stay but a little, I will come again.   *[Exit above.]*

        ROMEO

O blessed, blessed night! I am afeard,
Being in night, all this is but a dream,   140
Too flattering-sweet to be substantial.

                        [Re-enter Juliet above.]

        JULIET

Three words, dear Romeo, and good night indeed.
If that thy bent of love be honourable,
Thy purpose marriage, send me word to-morrow.
By one that I'll procure to come to thee,   145
Where and what time thou wilt perform the rite;
And all my fortunes at thy foot I'll lay,
And follow thee my lord throughout the world.

        NURSE [*within*]

Madam!

        JULIET

I come, anon.—But if thou meanest not well,   150
I do beseech thee—

        NURSE [*within*]

Madam!

        JULIET

           By and by, I come.—
To cease thy strife, and leave me to my grief.
To-morrow will I send.

        ROMEO

              So thrive my soul—

        JULIET

A thousand times good night.   *[Exit above.]* 155

        ROMEO

A thousand times the worse, to want thy light.
Love goes toward love as schoolboys from their books,
But love from love, toward school with heavy looks.

                        [Re-enter Juliet.]

        JULIET

Hist, Romeo, hist! O for a falconer's voice,

To lure this tassel-gentle back again.   160
Bondage is hoarse, and may not speak aloud,
Else would I tear the cave where Echo lies,
And make her airy tongue more hoarse than mine,
With repetition of my Romeo's name.
Romeo!

      ROMEO
It is my soul that calls upon my name.   165
How silver-sweet sound lovers' tongues by night,
Like softest music to attending ears.

      JULIET
Romeo!

      ROMEO
My sweet.

      JULIET
                At what a clock to-morrow
Shall I send to thee?

      ROMEO
                By the hour of nine.

      JULIET
I will not fail; 'tis twenty years till then.   170
I have forgot why I did call thee back.

      ROMEO
Let me stand here till thou remember it.

      JULIET
I shall forget, to have thee still stand there,
Remembering how I love thy company.

      ROMEO
And I'll still stay, to have thee still forget,   175
Forgetting any other home but this.

      JULIET
'Tis almost morning; I would have thee gone,
And yet no farther than a wanton's bird,
That lets it hop a little from her hand,
Like a poor prisoner in his twisted gyves,   180
And with a silken thread plucks it back again,
So loving-jealous of his liberty.

      ROMEO
I would I were thy bird.

JULIET

       Sweet, so would I;
Yet I should kill thee with much cherishing.
Good night, good night. Parting is such sweet sorrow,   185
That I shall say good night till it be morrow.

         [Exit above.]

ROMEO

Sleep dwell upon thine eyes, peace in thy breast.
Would I were sleep and peace, so sweet to rest.
Hence will I to my ghostly father's cell,
His help to crave, and my dear hap to tell.   190

         [Exit]

SCENE THREE.

Verona. Friar Laurence's cell.
Enter Friar Laurence, with a basket.

FRIAR LAURENCE

The gray-eyed morn smiles on the frowning night,
Check'ring the eastern clouds with streaks of light;
And fleckeled darkness like a drunkard reels
From forth day's path and Titan's fiery wheels.
Now ere the sun advance his burning eye,   5
The day to cheer, and night's dank dew to dry.
I must up-fill this osier-cage of ours
With baleful weeds and precious-juiced flowers.
The earth that's nature's mother is her tomb;
What is her burying grave, that is her womb.   10
And from her womb children of divers kind
We sucking on her natural bosom find;
Many for many virtues excellent,
None but for some, and yet all different.
O mickle is the powerful grace that lies   15
In plants, herbs, stones, and their true qualities.
For naught so vile that on the earth doth live,
But to the earth some special good doth give;

Nor aught so good, but strained from that fair use,
Revolts from true birth, stumbling on abuse.   20
Virtue itself turns vice being misapplied,
And vice sometime's by action dignified.
           [*Enter Romeo and stands by the door.*]
Within the infant rind of this weak flower
Poison hath residence, and medicine power;
For this being smelt with that part cheers each part;   25
Being tasted, slays all senses with the heart.
Two such opposed kings encamp them still
In man as well as herbs—grace and rude will;
And where the worser is predominant,
Full soon the canker death eats up that plant.   30

           R O M E O [*advances*]
Good morrow father.

           F R I A R   L A U R E N C E
                   Benedicite!
What early tongue so sweet saluteth me?
Young son, it argues a distempered head
So soon to bid good morrow to thy bed.
Care keeps his watch in every old man's eye,   35
And where care lodges, sleep will never lie;
But where unbruised youth with unstuffed brain
Doth couch his limbs, there golden sleep doth reign.
Therefore thy earliness doth me assure
Thou art up-roused by some distemperature;   40
Or if not so, then here I hit it right,
Our Romeo hath not been in bed to-night.

           R O M E O
That last is true; the sweeter rest was mine.

           F R I A R   L A U R E N C E
God pardon sin, wast thou with Rosaline?

           R O M E O
With Rosaline, my ghostly father, no.   45
I have forgot that name, and that name's woe.

           F R I A R   L A U R E N C E
That's my good son; but where hast thou been then?

           R O M E O
I'll tell thee ere thou ask it me again.
I have been feasting with mine enemy,

Where on a sudden one hath wounded me, 50
That's by me wounded; both our remedies
Within thy help and holy physic lies.
I bear no hatred, blessed man; for lo,
My intercession likewise steads my foe.

FRIAR LAURENCE

Be plain good son, and homely in thy drift; 55
Riddling confession finds but riddling shrift.

ROMEO

Then plainly know my heart's dear love is set
On the fair daughter of rich Capulet.
As mine on hers, so hers is set on mine,
And all combined, save what thou must combine 60
By holy marriage. When, and where, and how,
We met, we wooed, and made exchange of vow.
I'll tell thee as we pass, but this I pray,
That thou consent to marry us to-day.

FRIAR LAURENCE

Holy Saint Francis, what a change is here! 65
Is Rosaline that thou didst love so dear
So soon forsaken? Young men's love then lies
Not truly in their hearts, but in their eyes.
Jesu Maria, what a deal of brine
Hath washed thy sallow cheeks for Rosaline! 70
How much salt water thrown away in waste,
To season love, that of it doth not taste!
The sun not yet thy sighs from heaven clears,
Thy old groans yet ring in mine ancient ears.
Lo here upon thy cheek the stain doth sit 75
Of an old tear that is not washed off yet.
If e'er thou wast thyself, and these woes thine,
Thou and these woes were all for Rosaline.
And art thou changed? Pronounce this sentence then,
Women may fall, when there's no strength in men. 80

ROMEO

Thou chid'st me oft for loving Rosaline.

FRIAR LAURENCE

For doting, not for loving, pupil mine.

ROMEO

And bad'st me bury love.

FRIAR LAURENCE
                        Not in a grave,
To lay one in another out to have.
ROMEO
I pray thee chide me not, her I love now   85
Doth grace for grace, and love for love allow.
The other did not so.
FRIAR LAURENCE
                        Oh she knew well
Thy love did read by rote, that could not spell.
But come young waverer, come go with me,
In one respect I'll thy assistant be;   90
For this alliance may so happy prove,
To turn your households' rancour to pure love.
ROMEO
O let us hence, I stand on sudden haste.
FRIAR LAURENCE
Wisely and slow, they stumble that run fast.
                                        [*Exeunt.*]

SCENE FOUR.

*Verona. A street. Enter Benvolio
and Mercutio.*

MERCUTIO
Where the devil should this Romeo be?
Came he not home to-night?
BENVOLIO
Not to his father's; I spoke with his man.
MERCUTIO
Why that same pale hard-hearted wench, that Rosaline,
Torments him so, that he will sure run mad.   5
BENVOLIO
Tybalt, the kinsman to old Capulet,

Hath sent a letter to his father's house.

MERCUTIO

A challenge, on my life.

BENVOLIO

Romeo will answer it.

MERCUTIO

Any man that can write may answer a letter.   10

BENVOLIO

Nay, he will answer the letter's master, how he dares
being dared.

MERCUTIO

Alas poor Romeo, he is already dead, stabbed with a
white wench's black eye, run through the ear with a
love-song, the very pin of his heart cleft with the   15
blind bow-boy's butt-shaft; and is he a man to encounter Tybalt?

BENVOLIO

Why what is Tybalt?

MERCUTIO

More than Prince of Cats. O he's the courageous   20
captain of compliments. He fights as you sing prick-
song, keeps time, distance, and proportion; he rests his
minim rests, one, two, and the third in your bosom;
the very butcher of a silk button, a duellist, a duellist;
a gentleman of the very first house, of the first and   25
second cause. Ah the immortal passado, the punto reverso, the hay!

BENVOLIO

The what?

MERCUTIO

The pox of such antic lisping affecting fantasticoes,
these new tuners of accent! By Jesu a very good   30
blade—a very tall man—a very good whore! Why,
is not this a lamentable thing, grandsire, that we
should be thus afflicted with these strange flies, these
fashion-mongers, these pardon-me's, who stand so
much on the new form that they cannot sit at ease   35
on the old bench! O their bones, their bones!

[Enter Romeo.]

BENVOLIO
Here comes Romeo, here comes Romeo.

MERCUTIO
Without his roe, like a dried herring. O flesh, flesh,
how art thou fishified! Now is he for the numbers
that Petrarch flowed in; Laura to his lady was a
kitchen-wench, marry she had a better love to be-
rhyme her; Dido a dowdy, Cleopatra a gipsy, Helen
and Hero, hildings and harlots; Thisbe a gray eye or
so, but not to the purpose—Signior Romeo, bon jour.   45
There's a French salutation to your French slop. You
gave us the counterfeit fairly last night.

ROMEO
Good morrow to you both. What counterfeit did I
give you?   50

MERCUTIO
The slip sir, the slip, can you not conceive?

ROMEO
Pardon good Mercutio, my business was great, and
in such a case as mine a man may strain courtesy.   55

MERCUTIO
That's as much as to say, such a case as yours
constrains a man to bow in the hams.

ROMEO
Meaning to curtsy.

MERCUTIO
Thou hast most kindly hit it.

ROMEO
A most courteous exposition.   60

MERCUTIO
Nay I am the very pink of courtesy.

ROMEO
Pink for flower.

MERCUTIO
Right.

ROMEO
Why then is my pump well flowered.

MERCUTIO
Sure wit. Follow me this jest now, till thou hast   65

worn out thy pump, that when the single sole of
it is worn, the jest may remain after the wearing
solely singular.

ROMEO

O single-soled jest, solely singular for the single-
ness.   70

MERCUTIO

Come between us good Benvolio; my wits faints.

ROMEO

Switch and spurs, switch and spurs; or I'll cry a
match.

MERCUTIO

Nay, if our wits run the wild-goose chase, I am   75
done; for thou hast more of the wild goose in one
of thy wits than I am sure I have in my whole five.
Was I with you there for the goose?

ROMEO

Thou wast never with me for anything, when thou
wast not there for the goose.   80

MERCUTIO

I will bite thee by the ear for that jest.

ROMEO

Nay good goose, bite not.

MERCUTIO

Thy wit is very bitter sweeting, it is most sharp
sauce.

ROMEO

And is it not then well served in to a sweet goose?   85

MERCUTIO

O here's a wit of cheveril, that stretches from an inch
narrow to an ell broad.

ROMEO

I stretch it out for that word broad, which added to
the goose proves thee far and wide a broad goose.   90

MERCUTIO

Why, is not this better now than groaning for love?
Now art thou sociable, now art thou Romeo; now
art thou what thou art, by art as well as by nature, for
this drivelling love is like a great natural that runs   95
lolling up and down to hide his bauble in a hole.

BENVOLIO

Stop there, stop there.

MERCUTIO

Thou desirest me to stop in my tale against the hair. 100

BENVOLIO

Thou wouldest else have made thy tale large.

MERCUTIO

O thou art deceived; I would have made it short, for
I was come to the whole depth of my tale, and meant
indeed to occupy the argument no longer. 105

[*Enter Nurse and Peter.*]

ROMEO

Here's goodly gear! A sail, a sail!

MERCUTIO

Two, two; a shirt and a smock.

NURSE

Peter. 110

PETER

Anon.

NURSE

My fan Peter.

MERCUTIO

Good Peter, to hide her face, for her fan's the fairer
face.

NURSE

God ye good morrow gentlemen. 115

MERCUTIO

God ye good den fair gentlewoman.

NURSE

Is it good den?

MERCUTIO

'Tis no less, I tell ye, for the bawdy hand of the dial
is now upon the prick of noon.

NURSE

Out upon you, what a man are you! 120

ROMEO

One, gentlewoman, that God hath made for himself
to mar.

NURSE

By my troth it is well said, for himself to mar quoth

'a? Gentlemen, can any of you tell me where I may
find the young Romeo?   125

NURSE

ROMEO

I can tell you, but young Romeo will be older when
you have found him than he was when you sought
him. I am the youngest of that name, for fault of a
worse.

NURSE

You say well.   130

MERCUTIO

Yea, is the worst well? Very well took, i' faith, wisely,
wisely.

NURSE

If you be he sir, I desire some confidence with you.

BENVOLIO

She will indite him to some supper.   135

MERCUTIO

A bawd, a bawd, a bawd! So ho!

ROMEO

What hast thou found?

MERCUTIO

No hare sir, unless a hare sir, in a Lenten pie, that
is something stale and hoar ere it be spent.

[Sings.] 140

> An old hare hoar,
> And an old hare hoar,
> Is very good meat in Lent.
> But a hare that is hoar
> Is too much for a score,   145
> When it hoars ere it be spent.

Romeo, will you come to your father's? We'll to
dinner thither.

ROMEO

I will follow you.

MERCUTIO

Farewell ancient lady; farewell, [sings] Lady, lady,   150
lady.

[Exeunt Mercutio and Benvolio.]

NURSE

I pray you sir, what saucy merchant was this that was
so full of his ropery?

ROMEO

A gentleman, nurse, that loves to hear himself talk,   155
and will speak more in a minute than he will stand to
in a month.

NURSE

An 'a speak any thing against me, I'll take him down,
an 'a were lustier than he is, and twenty such Jacks;
and if I cannot, I'll find those that shall. Scurvy   160
knave, I am none of his flirt-gills, I am none of his
skains-mates. [To Peter.] And thou must stand by
too and suffer every knave to use me at his pleasure?

PETER

I saw no man use you at his pleasure; if I had, my   165
weapon should quickly have been out, I warrant you:
I dare draw as soon as another man, if I see occasion
in a good quarrel, and the law on my side.

NURSE

Now afore God I am so vexed, that every part   170
about me quivers. Scurvy knave! Pray you sir a
word: and as I told you, my young lady bid me
enquire you out; what she bid me say, I will keep
to myself; but first let me tell ye, if ye should lead
her in a fool's paradise, as they say, it were a very   175
gross kind of behaviour, as they say; for the gentlewoman is young; and therefore, if you should deal
double with her, truly it were an ill thing to be offered
to any gentlewoman, and very weak dealing.   180

ROMEO

Nurse, commend me to thy lady and mistress. I protest
unto thee—

NURSE

Good heart, and i' faith I will tell her as much. Lord,
lord, she will be a joyful woman.   185

ROMEO

What wilt thou tell her, nurse? Thou dost not mark
me.

NURSE

I will tell her sir, that you do protest, which as I take
it is a gentlemanlike offer.   190

ROMEO

Bid her devise
Some means to come to shrift this afternoon,
And there she shall at Friar Laurence' cell
Be shrived and married. Here is for thy pains.

NURSE

No truly sir, not a penny.   195

ROMEO

Go to, I say you shall.

NURSE

This afternoon sir? Well, she shall be there.

ROMEO

And stay good nurse behind the abbey wall,
Within this hour my man shall be with thee,   200
And bring thee cords made like a tackled stair,
Which to the high top-gallant of my joy
Must be my convoy in the secret night.
Farewell; be trusty, and I'll quit thy pains.
Farewell, commend me to thy mistress.   205

NURSE

Now God in heaven bless thee. Hark you sir.

ROMEO

What sayst thou my dear nurse?

NURSE

Is your man secret? Did you ne'er hear say,
Two may keep counsel, putting one away?

ROMEO

I warrant thee my man's as true as steel.   210

NURSE

Well sir, my mistress is the sweetest lady. Lord, lord,
when 'twas a little prating thing. O there is a nobleman
in town, one Paris, that would fain lay knife aboard;
but she good soul had as lief see a toad, a very toad,
as see him. I anger her sometimes, and tell her that   215
Paris is the properer man, but I'll warrant you, when
I say so, she looks as pale as any clout in the versal

world. Doth not rosemary and Romeo begin both
with a letter?   220

ROMEO

Ay nurse, what of that? Both with an R.

NURSE

Ah mocker, that's the dog's name; R is for the—
no, I know it begins with some other letter. And she
hath the prettiest sententious of it, of you and rose-   225
mary, that it would do you good to hear it.

ROMEO

Commend me to thy lady.

NURSE

Ay, a thousand times. [*Exit Romeo.*] Peter!   230

PETER

Anon.

NURSE [*gives him her fan to carry*]

Before, and apace.   [*Exeunt.*]

SCENE FIVE.

Verona. Capulet's orchard.
Enter Juliet.

JULIET

The clock struck nine when I did send the nurse;
In half an hour she promised to return.
Perchance she cannot meet him—that's not so—
O she is lame, love's heralds should be thoughts,
Which ten times faster glide than the sun's beams,   5
Driving back shadows over louring hills.
Therefore do nimble-pinioned doves draw love,
And therefore hath the wind-swift Cupid wings.
Now is the sun upon the highmost hill

Of this day's journey, and from nine till twelve   10
Is three long hours, yet she is not come.
Had she affections and warm youthful blood,
She would be as swift in motion as a ball;
My words would bandy her to my sweet love,
And his to me.   15
But old folks, many feign as they were dead,
Unwieldy, slow, heavy and pale as lead.

                        [*Enter Nurse and Peter.*]

O God she comes! O honey nurse what news?
Hast thou met with him? Send thy man away.

          NURSE
Peter, stay at the gate.   [*Exit Peter.*] 20

          JULIET
Now good sweet nurse—o lord, why look'st thou sad?
Though news be sad, yet tell them merrily.
If good, thou sham'st the music of sweet news,
By playing it to me with so sour a face.

          NURSE
I am aweary, give me leave awhile.   25
Fie how my bones ache, what a jaunce have I had!

          JULIET
I would thou hadst my bones, and I thy news.
Nay come I pray thee speak, good, good nurse speak.

          NURSE
Jesu, what haste! Can you not stay awhile?
Do you not see that I am out of breath?   30

          JULIET
How art thou out of breath, when thou hast breath
To say to me that thou art out of breath?
The excuse that thou dost make in this delay
Is longer than the tale thou dost excuse.
Is thy news good or bad? Answer to that.   35
Say either, and I'll stay the circumstance.
Let me be satisfied, is't good or bad?

          NURSE
Well, you have made a simple choice, you know
not how to choose a man. Romeo? No, not he, though
his face be better than any man's, yet his leg excels   40
all men's; and for a hand and a foot and a body,

though they be not to be talked on, yet they are past
compare. He is not the flower of courtesy, but I'll
warrant him, as gentle as a lamb. Go thy ways wench,
serve God. What, have you dined at home?   45

JULIET

No, no. But all this did I know before.
What says he of our marriage, what of that?

NURSE

Lord how my head aches, what a head have I!
It beats as it would fall in twenty pieces.   50
My back a tother side, ah my back, my back!
Beshrew your heart for sending me about
To catch my death with jauncing up and down.

JULIET

I' faith I am sorry that thou art not well.
Sweet, sweet, sweet nurse, tell me what says my love?   55

NURSE

Your love says, like an honest gentleman, and a
courteous, and a kind, and a handsome, and I warrant
a virtuous—where is your mother?

JULIET

Where is my mother? Why she is within,   60
Where should she be? How oddly thou repliest!
Your love says like an honest gentleman,
Where is your mother?

NURSE

                    O God's lady dear,
Are you so hot? Marry come up I trow,
Is this the poultice for my aching bones?   65
Henceforward do your messages yourself.

JULIET

Here's such a coil. Come, what says Romeo?

NURSE

Have you got leave to go to shrift to-day?

JULIET

I have.

NURSE

Then hie you hence to Friar Laurence' cell,   70
There stays a husband to make you a wife.
Now comes the wanton blood up in your cheeks,

They'll be in scarlet straight at any news.
Hie you to church. I must another way,
To fetch a ladder by the which your love   75
Must climb a bird's nest soon when it is dark.
I am the drudge, and toil in your delight.
But you shall bear the burden soon at night.
Go. I'll to dinner. Hie you to the cell.
        JULIET
Hie to high fortune! Honest nurse farewell.   80

                              [*Exeunt.*]

        SCENE SIX.

        Verona. Friar Laurence's cell.
        Enter Friar Laurence and Romeo.

        FRIAR LAURENCE
So smile the heavens upon this holy act,
That after-hours with sorrow chide us not.
        ROMEO
Amen, amen, but come what sorrow can,
It cannot countervail the exchange of joy
That one short minute gives me in her sight.   5
Do thou but close our hands with holy words,
Then love-devouring death do what he dare,
It is enough I may but call her mine.
        FRIAR LAURENCE
These violent delights have violent ends,
And in their triumph die; like fire and powder,   10
Which as they kiss consume. The sweetest honey
Is loathsome in his own deliciousness,
And in the taste confounds the appetite.
Therefore love moderately, long love doth so;
Too swift arrives as tardy as too slow. [*Enter Juliet.*] 15
Here comes the lady. O so light a foot
Will ne'er wear out the everlasting flint.
A lover may bestride the gossamers

That idles in the wanton summer air,
And yet not fall; so light is vanity.   20
    JULIET
Good even to my ghostly confessor.
    FRIAR LAURENCE
Romeo shall thank thee daughter for us both.
    JULIET
As much to him, else is his thanks too much.
    ROMEO
Ah, Juliet, if the measure of thy joy
Be heaped like mine, and that thy skill be more   25
To blazon it, then sweeten with thy breath
This neighbour air, and let rich music's tongue
Unfold the imagined happiness that both
Receive in either by this dear encounter.
    JULIET
Conceit, more rich in matter than in words,   30
Brags of his substance, not of ornament.
They are but beggars that can count their worth.
But my true love is grown to such excess,
I cannot sum up sum of half my wealth.
    FRIAR LAURENCE
Come, come with me, and we will make short work.   35
For by your leaves, you shall not stay alone,
Till holy Church incorporate two in one.   [Exeunt.]

ACT III

SCENE ONE.

Verona. A public place. Enter Mercutio,
Benvolio, Page, and Servants.

BENVOLIO

I pray thee good Mercutio, let's retire.
The day is hot, the Capulets abroad;
And if we meet we shall not 'scape a brawl,
For now these hot days, is the mad blood stirring.

MERCUTIO

Thou art like one of these fellows that when he enters   5
the confines of a tavern claps me his sword upon the
table, and says, God send me no need of thee; and by
the operation of the second cup draws him on the
drawer, when indeed there is no need. ──────   10

BENVOLIO

Am I like such a fellow?

MERCUTIO

Come, come, thou art as hot a Jack in thy mood
as any in Italy; and as soon moved to be moody, and
as soon moody to be moved.

BENVOLIO

And what to?   15

MERCUTIO

Nay an there were two such we should have none
shortly, for one would kill the other. Thou? Why thou
wilt quarrel with a man that hath a hair more, or a
hair less, in his beard than thou hast; thou wilt quarrel
with a man for cracking nuts, having no other reason   20

but because thou hast hazel eyes; what eye, but such
an eye, would spy out such a quarrel? Thy head is
as full of quarrels as an egg is full of meat, and yet
thy head hath been beaten as addle as an egg for   25
quarrelling. Thou hast quarrelled with a man for
coughing in the street, because he hath wakened thy
dog that hath lain asleep in the sun. Didst thou not
fall out with a tailor for wearing his new doublet   30
before Easter? With another for tying his new shoes
with old riband? And yet thou wilt tutor me from
quarrelling.

    B E N V O L I O

An I were so apt to quarrel as thou art, any man
should buy the fee-simple of my life for an hour and   35
a quarter.

    M E R C U T I O

The fee-simple? O simple!

    [*Enter Tybalt, Petruchio, and other Capulets.*]

    B E N V O L I O

By my head, here comes the Capulets.

    M E R C U T I O

By my heel, I care not.

    T Y B A L T

Follow me close, for I will speak to them. Gentle-   40
men, good den; a word with one of you.

    M E R C U T I O

And but one word with one of us? Couple it with
something, make it a word and a blow.

    T Y B A L T

You shall find me apt enough to that sir, an you will
give me occasion.   45

    M E R C U T I O

Could you not take some occasion without giving?

    T Y B A L T

Mercutio, thou consortest with Romeo.

    M E R C U T I O

Consort? What, dost thou make us minstrels? An
thou make minstrels of us, look to hear nothing but   50
discords. Here's my fiddlestick, here's that shall make
you dance. Zounds, consort!

BENVOLIO

We talk here in the public haunt of men.
Either withdraw unto some private place,
Or reason coldly of your grievances,   55
Or else depart; here all eyes gaze on us.

MERCUTIO

Men's eyes were made to look, and let them gaze.
I will not budge for no man's pleasure, I.
                                   [*Enter Romeo.*]

TYBALT

Well, peace be with you sir, here comes my man.

MERCUTIO

But I'll be hanged sir, if he wear your livery.   60
Marry go before to field, he'll be your follower;
Your worship in that sense may call him man.

TYBALT

Romeo, the love I bear thee can afford
No better term than this—thou art a villain.

ROMEO

Tybalt, the reason that I have to love thee   65
Doth much excuse the appertaining rage
To such a greeting—villain am I none.
Therefore farewell, I see thou knowest me not.

TYBALT

Boy, this shall not excuse the injuries
That thou hast done me, therefore turn and draw.   70

ROMEO

I do protest I never injured thee,
But love thee better than thou canst devise,
Till thou shalt know the reason of my love.
And so good Capulet, which name I tender
As dearly as mine own, be satisfied.   75

MERCUTIO

O calm, dishonourable, vile submission!
Alla stoccata carries it away.   [*Draws.*]
Tybalt, you rat-catcher, will you walk?

TYBALT

What wouldst thou have with me?

MERCUTIO

Good King of Cats, nothing but one of your nine   80

lives, that I mean to make bold withal, and as you
shall use me hereafter dry-beat the rest of the eight.
Will you pluck your sword out of his pilcher by
the ears? Make haste, lest mine be about your ears
ere it be out.   85

    TYBALT

I am for you.   [*Draws.*]

    ROMEO

Gentle Mercutio, put thy rapier up.

    MERCUTIO

Come sir, your passado.   [*They fight.*]

    ROMEO

Draw Benvolio, beat down their weapons.
Gentlemen, for shame, forbear this outrage.   90
Tybalt, Mercutio, the Prince expressly hath
Forbid this bandying in Verona streets.
Hold Tybalt. Good Mercutio—

    [*Tybalt thrusts Mercutio, and exits with other
    Capulets.*]

    MERCUTIO

                  I am hurt.
A plague a both your houses, I am sped.
Is he gone and hath nothing?

    BENVOLIO

              What, art thou hurt?   95

    MERCUTIO

Ay, ay, a scratch, a scratch; marry 'tis enough.
Where is my page? Go villain, fetch a surgeon.

                  [*Exit Page.*]

    ROMEO

Courage man, the hurt cannot be much.

    MERCUTIO

No 'tis not so deep as a well, nor so wide as a church
door, but 'tis enough, 'twill serve. Ask for me to-   100
morrow, and you shall find me a grave man. I am
peppered, I warrant, for this world. A plague a both
your houses! Zounds, a dog, a rat, a mouse, a cat, to
scratch a man to death! A braggart, a rogue, a villain,
that fights by the book of arithmetic! Why the devil   105

came you between us? I was hurt under your arm.

ROMEO

I thought it all for the best.

MERCUTIO

Help me into some house Benvolio,   110
Or I shall faint. A plague a both your houses!
They have made worms' meat of me. I have it,
And soundly too. Your houses!

[*Exit, led by Benvolio and Servants.*]

ROMEO

This gentleman, the Prince's near ally,
My very friend, hath got this mortal hurt   115
In my behalf; my reputation stained
With Tybalt's slander, Tybalt that an hour
Hath been my cousin. O sweet Juliet,
Thy beauty hath made me effeminate,
And in my temper softened valour's steel.   120

[*Enter Benvolio.*]

BENVOLIO

O Romeo, Romeo, brave Mercutio is dead.
That gallant spirit hath aspired the clouds,
Which too untimely here did scorn the earth.

ROMEO

This day's black fate on more days doth depend,
This but begins the woe others must end.   125

[*Enter Tybalt.*]

BENVOLIO

Here comes the furious Tybalt back again.

ROMEO

Again? In triumph! And Mercutio slain.
Away to heaven respective lenity,
And fire-eyed fury be my conduct now
Now Tybalt take the villain back again   130
That late thou gavest me, for Mercutio's soul
Is but a little way above our heads,
Staying for thine to keep him company.
Either thou or I, or both, must go with him.

TYBALT

Thou wretched boy, that didst consort him here,   135
Shalt with him hence.

ROMEO

     This shall determine that.
      [They fight; Tybalt falls.]

BENVOLIO

Romeo away, be gone.
The citizens are up, and Tybalt slain.
Stand not amazed, the Prince will doom thee death,
If thou art taken. Hence, be gone, away.   140

ROMEO

O I am fortune's fool!

BENVOLIO

      Why dost thou stay?
      [Exit Romeo. Enter citizens.]

CITIZEN

Which way ran he that killed Mercutio?
Tybalt, that murderer, which way ran he?

BENVOLIO

There lies that Tybalt.

CITIZEN

     Up sir, go with me.
I charge thee in the Prince's name obey.   145
   *[Enter Prince, Montague, Capulet, Lady Mon-
   tague and Lady Capulet, attended.]*

PRINCE

Where are the vile beginners of this fray?

BENVOLIO

O noble Prince, I can discover all
The unlucky manage of this fatal brawl.
There lies the man, slain by young Romeo,
That slew thy kinsman, brave Mercutio.   150

LADY CAPULET

Tybalt, my cousin, o my brother's child!
O Prince, o cousin, husband! O the blood is spilt
Of my dear kinsman! Prince, as thou art true,
For blood of ours shed blood of Montague.
O cousin, cousin!   155

PRINCE

Benvolio, who began this bloody fray?

BENVOLIO

Tybalt here slain, whom Romeo's hand did slay.

Romeo, that spoke him fair, bid him bethink
How nice the quarrel was, and urged withal
Your high displeasure. All this, uttered   160
With gentle breath, calm look, knees humbly bowed,
Could not take truce with the unruly spleen
Of Tybalt deaf to peace, but that he tilts
With piercing steel at bold Mercutio's breast;
Who, all as hot, turns deadly point to point,   165
And with a martial scorn, with one hand beats
Cold death aside, and with the other sends
It back to Tybalt, whose dexterity
Retorts it. Romeo he cries aloud,
Hold friends, friends part, and swifter than his tongue,   170
His agile arm beats down their fatal points,
And 'twixt them rushes; underneath whose arm
An envious thrust from Tybalt hit the life
Of stout Mercutio, and then Tybalt fled;
But by and by comes back to Romeo,   175
Who had but newly entertained revenge,
And to't they go like lightning, for ere I
Could draw to part them was stout Tybalt slain.
And as he fell, did Romeo turn and fly.
This is the truth, or let Benvolio die.   180

        LADY CAPULET
He is a kinsman to the Montague;
Affection makes him false, he speaks not true.
Some twenty of them fought in this black strife,
And all those twenty could but kill one life.
I beg for justice, which thou, Prince, must give.   185
Romeo slew Tybalt, Romeo must not live.

        PRINCE
Romeo slew him, he slew Mercutio.
Who now the price of his dear blood doth owe?

        MONTAGUE
Not Romeo, Prince, he was Mercutio's friend;
His fault concludes but what the law should end,   190
The life of Tybalt.

        PRINCE
                And for that offence
Immediately we do exile him hence.

I have an interest in your hate's proceeding:
My blood for your rude brawls doth lie a-bleeding.
But I'll amerce you with so strong a fine,   195
That you shall all repent the loss of mine.
I will be deaf to pleading and excuses,
Nor tears nor prayers shall purchase out abuses.
Therefore use none. Let Romeo hence in haste,
Else, when he is found, that hour is his last.   200
Bear hence this body, and attend our will.
Mercy but murders, pardoning those that kill.

[Exeunt.]

SCENE TWO.

Verona. Capulet's orchard. Enter Juliet.

JULIET

Gallop apace, you fiery-footed steeds,
Towards Phoebus' lodging; such a wagoner
As Phaethon would whip you to the west,
And bring in cloudy night immediately.
Spread thy close curtain, love-performing night,   5
That runaway's eyes may wink, and Romeo
Leap to these arms, untalked of and unseen.
Lovers can see to do their amorous rites,
And by their own beauties; or if love be blind,
It best agrees with night. Come civil night,   10
Thou sober-suited matron all in black,
And learn me how to lose a winning match,
Played for a pair of stainless maidenhoods.
Hood my unmanned blood bating in my cheeks
With thy black mantle, till strange love grow bold,   15
Think true love acted simple modesty.
Come night, come Romeo, come thou day in night;
For thou wilt lie upon the wings of night,
Whiter than new snow upon a raven's back.
Come gentle night, come loving black-browed night,   20
Give me my Romeo, and when he shall die,

Take him and cut him out in little stars,
And he will make the face of heaven so fine,
That all the world will be in love with night,
And pay no worship to the garish sun.   25
O I have brought the mansion of a love,
But not possessed it, and though I am sold,
Not yet enjoyed. So tedious is this day,
As is the night before some festival
To an impatient child that hath new robes   30
And may not wear them.

> [Enter Nurse with ladder of cords.]
>   O here comes my nurse.

And she brings news; and every tongue that speaks
But Romeo's name speaks heavenly eloquence.
Now nurse, what news? What, hast thou there the
  cords
That Romeo bid thee fetch?

NURSE

>   Ay, ay, the cords.   35
>   [Throws them down.]

JULIET

Ay me, what news? Why dost thou wring thy hands?

NURSE

Ah weladay, he's dead, he's dead, he's dead.
We are undone lady, we are undone.
Alack the day, he's gone, he's killed, he's dead.

JULIET

Can heaven be so envious?

NURSE

>   Romeo can,   40

Though heaven cannot. O Romeo, Romeo,
Who ever would have thought it? Romeo!

JULIET

What devil art thou, that dost torment me thus?
This torture should be roared in dismal hell.
Hath Romeo slain himself? Say thou but ay,   45
And that bare vowel I shall poison more
Than the death-darting eye of cockatrice.
I am not I, if there be such an I;
Or those eyes shut that makes thee answer ay.

If he be slain, say ay, or if not, no,   50
Brief sounds determine of my weal or woe.

NURSE

I saw the wound, I saw it with mine eyes—
God save the mark—here on his manly breast.
A piteous corse, a bloody piteous corse,
Pale, pale as ashes, all bedaubed in blood,   55
All in gore-blood. I swounded at the sight.

JULIET

O break, my heart, poor bankrupt, break at once.
To prison eyes, ne'er look on liberty.
Vile earth, to earth resign; end motion here;
And thou and Romeo press one heavy bier.   60

NURSE

O Tybalt, Tybalt, the best friend I had,
O courteous Tybalt, honest gentleman,
That ever I should live to see thee dead!

JULIET

What storm is this that blows so contrary?
Is Romeo slaughtered? And is Tybalt dead?   65
My dearest cousin, and my dearer lord?
Then dreadful trumpet, sound the general doom,
For who is living, if those two are gone?

NURSE

Tybalt is gone, and Romeo banished.
Romeo that killed him, he is banished.   70

JULIET

O God, did Romeo's hand shed Tybalt's blood?

NURSE

It did, it did, alas the day, it did!

JULIET

O serpent heart, hid with a flow'ring face!
Did ever dragon keep so fair a cave?
Beautiful tyrant, fiend angelical,   75
Dove-feathered raven, wolvish-ravening lamb,
Despised substance of divinest show,
Just opposite to what thou justly seem'st,
A damned saint, an honourable villain!
O nature, what hadst thou to do in hell,   80
When thou didst bower the spirit of a fiend

In mortal paradise of such sweet flesh?
Was ever book containing such vile matter
So fairly bound? O that deceit should dwell
In such a gorgeous palace!

NURSE

                There's no trust,   85
No faith, no honesty in men; all perjured,
All forsworn, all naught, all dissemblers.
Ah, where's my man? Give me some aqua-vitae.
These griefs, these woes, these sorrows make me old.
Shame come to Romeo.

JULIET

                Blistered be thy tongue   90
For such a wish. He was not born to shame.
Upon his brow shame is ashamed to sit;
For 'tis a throne where honour may be crowned
Sole monarch of the universal earth.
O what a beast was I to chide at him!   95

NURSE

Will you speak well of him that killed your cousin?

JULIET

Shall I speak ill of him that is my husband?
Ah poor my lord, what tongue shall smooth thy name,
When I thy three-hours wife have mangled it?
But wherefore, villain, didst thou kill my cousin?   100
That villain cousin would have killed my husband.
Back foolish tears, back to your native spring,
Your tributary drops belong to woe,
Which you mistaking offer up to joy.
My husband lives, that Tybalt would have slain,   105
And Tybalt's dead, that would have slain my husband.
All this is comfort, wherefore weep I then?
Some word there was, worser than Tybalt's death,
That murdered me, I would forget it fain;
But o it presses to my memory,   110
Like damned guilty deeds to sinners' minds.
Tybalt is dead and Romeo banished.
That banished, that one word banished,
Hath slain ten thousand Tybalts. Tybalt's death
Was woe enough if it had ended there.   115

Or, if sour woe delights in fellowship,
And needly will be ranked with other griefs,
Why followed not, when she said Tybalt's dead,
Thy father or thy mother, nay or both,
Which modern lamentation might have moved?   120
But with a rearward following Tybalt's death,
Romeo is banished—to speak that word,
Is father, mother, Tybalt, Romeo, Juliet,
All slain, all dead. Romeo is banished.
There is no end, no limit, measure, bound,   125
In that word's death; no words can that woe sound.
Where is my father and my mother, nurse?

NURSE

Weeping and wailing over Tybalt's corse.
Will you go to them? I will bring you thither.

JULIET

Wash they his wounds with tears? Mine shall be spent,   130
When theirs are dry, for Romeo's banishment.
Take up those cords. Poor ropes you are beguiled,
Both you and I, for Romeo is exiled.
He made you for a highway to my bed,
But I a maid die maiden-widowed.   135
Come cords, come nurse, I'll to my wedding-bed,
And death, not Romeo, take my maidenhead.

NURSE

Hie to your chamber, I'll find Romeo
To comfort you. I wot well where he is.
Hark ye, your Romeo will be here at night.   140
I'll to him, he is hid at Laurence' cell.

JULIET

O find him, give this ring to my true knight,
And bid him come, to take his last farewell.

[Exeunt.]

SCENE THREE.

Verona. Friar Laurence's cell.
Enter Friar Laurence.

FRIAR LAURENCE
Romeo come forth, come forth thou fearful man.
Affliction is enamoured of thy parts,
And thou art wedded to calamity.   [*Enter Romeo.*]

ROMEO
Father what news? What is the Prince's doom?
What sorrow craves acquaintance at my hand,   5
That I yet know not?
      FRIAR LAURENCE
               Too familiar
Is my dear son with such sour company.
I bring thee tidings of the Prince's doom.
      ROMEO
What less than doomsday is the Prince's doom?
      FRIAR LAURENCE
A gentler judgement vanished from his lips;   10
Not body's death, but body's banishment.
      ROMEO
Ha, banishment? Be merciful, say death;
For exile hath more terror in his look,
Much more than death. Do not say banishment.
      FRIAR LAURENCE
Hence from Verona art thou banished.   15
Be patient, for the world is broad and wide.
      ROMEO
There is no world without Verona walls,
But purgatory, torture, hell itself.
Hence banished is banished from the world,
And world's exile is death. Then banished   20
Is death mis-termed. Calling death banished,
Thou cut'st my head off with a golden axe,
And smilest upon the stroke that murders me.
      FRIAR LAURENCE
O deadly sin, o rude unthankfulness!

Thy fault our law calls death, but the kind Prince   25
Taking thy part hath rushed aside the law,
And turned that black word death to banishment.
This is dear mercy, and thou seest it not.

ROMEO

'Tis torture and not mercy; heaven is here
Where Juliet lives; and every cat and dog,   30
And little mouse, every unworthy thing,
Live here in heaven, and may look on her,
But Romeo may not. More validity,
More honourable state, more courtship lives
In carrion flies than Romeo; they may seize   35
On the white wonder of dear Juliet's hand,
And steal immortal blessing from her lips,
Who even in pure and vestal modesty
Still blush, as thinking their own kisses sin.*
But Romeo may not, he is banished.   40
Flies may do this, but I from this must fly;
They are freemen, but I am banished.
Hadst thou no poison mixed, no sharp-ground knife,
No sudden mean of death, though ne'er so mean,   45
But—banished—to kill me? Banished?
O friar, the damned use that word in hell;
Howling attends it. How hast thou the heart,
Being a divine, a ghostly confessor,
A sin-absolver, and my friend professed,   50
To mangle me with that word banished?
This may flies do, when I from this must fly,
And sayest thou yet, that exile is not death?

FRIAR LAURENCE

Thou fond mad man, hear me a little speak.

ROMEO

O thou wilt speak again of banishment.

FRIAR LAURENCE

I'll give thee armour to keep off that word,
Adversity's sweet milk, philosophy,   55
To comfort thee though thou art banished.

---

*Lines deleted in rewriting:

ROMEO

Yet banished? Hang up philosophy,
Unless philosophy can make a Juliet,
Displant a town, reverse a Prince's doom,
It helps not, it prevails not. Talk no more.   60

FRIAR LAURENCE

O then I see that mad men have no ears.

ROMEO

How should they when that wise men have no eyes?

FRIAR LAURENCE

Let me dispute with thee of thy estate.

ROMEO

Thou canst not speak of that thou dost not feel.
Wert thou as young as I, Juliet thy love,   65
An hour but married, Tybalt murdered,
Doting like me, and like me banished,
Then mightst thou speak, then mightst thou tear thy
    hair,
And fall upon the ground, as I do now,
Taking the measure of an unmade grave.   70

[*Nurse within knocks.*]

FRIAR LAURENCE

Arise. One knocks; good Romeo hide thyself.

ROMEO

Not I, unless the breath of heart-sick groans
Mist-like infold me from the search of eyes.

[*She knocks again.*]

FRIAR LAURENCE

Hark how they knock.—Who's there?—Romeo arise;
Thou wilt be taken.—Stay awhile.—Stand up.   75

[*Knock.*]

Run to my study.—By and by.—God's will,
What simpleness is this!—I come, I come.

[*Knock.*]

Who knocks so hard? Whence come you? What's your
    will?

NURSE [*within*]

Let me come in, and you shall know my errand.
I come from Lady Juliet.

Thou pouts upon thy fortune and thy love.
Take heed, take heed, for such die miserable.   145
Go get thee to thy love as was decreed,
Ascend her chamber, hence and comfort her;
But look thou stay not till the watch be set,
For then thou canst not pass to Mantua,
Where thou shalt live till we can find a time   150
To blaze your marriage, reconcile your friends,
Beg pardon of the Prince, and call thee back,
With twenty hundred thousand times more joy
Than thou went'st forth in lamentation.
Go before nurse, commend me to thy lady,   155
And bid her hasten all the house to bed,
Which heavy sorrow makes them apt unto.
Romeo is coming.
        NURSE
O lord, I could have stayed here all the night
To hear good counsel. O what learning is!   160
My lord, I'll tell my lady you will come.
        ROMEO
Do so, and bid my sweet prepare to chide.
        NURSE
Here sir, a ring she bid me give you, sir.
Hie you, make haste, for it grows very late.   [Exit.]
        ROMEO
How well my comfort is revived by this!   165
        FRIAR LAURENCE
Go hence; good night; and here stands all your state—
Either be gone before the watch be set,
Or by the break of day disguised from hence.
Sojourn in Mantua; I'll find out your man,
And he shall signify from time to time   170
Every good hap to you that chances here.
Give me thy hand, 'tis late. Farewell; good night.
        ROMEO
But that a joy past joy calls out on me,
It were a grief, so brief to part with thee.
Farewell.   [Exeunt.]   175

SCENE FOUR.

Verona. A hall in Capulet's house.
Enter Capulet, Lady Capulet, and Paris.

CAPULET

Things have fall'n out sir so unluckily,
That we have had no time to move our daughter.
Look you, she loved her kinsman Tybalt dearly,
And so did I. Well, we were born to die.
'Tis very late, she'll not come down to-night. 5
I promise you, but for your company,
I would have been abed an hour ago.

PARIS

These times of woe afford no time to woo.
Madam good night, commend me to your daughter.

LADY CAPULET

I will, and know her mind early to-morrow; 10
To-night she's mewed up to her heaviness.

CAPULET

Sir Paris, I will make a desperate tender
Of my child's love. I think she will be ruled
In all respects by me; nay more, I doubt it not.
Wife, go you to her ere you go to bed, 15
Acquaint her here of my son Paris' love,
And bid her, mark you me, on Wednesday next—
But soft, what day is this?

PARIS

Monday my lord.

CAPULET

Monday? Ha, ha, well Wednesday is too soon.
A Thursday let it be, a Thursday, tell her, 20
She shall be married to this noble earl.
Will you be ready? Do you like this haste?
We'll keep no great ado—a friend or two.
For hark you, Tybalt being slain so late,
It may be thought we held him carelessly, 25

Being our kinsman, if we revel much.
Therefore we'll have some half a dozen friends,
And there an end. But what say you to Thursday?
            PARIS
My lord, I would that Thursday were to-morrow.
            CAPULET
Well get you gone, a Thursday be it then.   30
Go you to Juliet ere you go to bed;
Prepare her, wife, against this wedding-day.
Farewell my lord. Light to my chamber ho!
Afore me, it is so very late, that we
May call it early by and by. Good night.   35

                              [*Exeunt.*]

SCENE FIVE.

Verona. Juliet's chamber.
Enter Romeo and Juliet above.

            JULIET
Wilt thou be gone? It is not yet near day.
It was the nightingale, and not the lark,
That pierced the fearful hollow of thine ear;
Nightly she sings on yond pomegranate tree.
Believe me love, it was the nightingale.   5
            ROMEO
It was the lark, the herald of the morn,
No nightingale. Look love, what envious streaks
Do lace the severing clouds in yonder east.
Night's candles are burnt out, and jocund day
Stands tiptoe on the misty mountain tops.   10
I must be gone and live, or stay and die.
            JULIET
Yond light is not day-light, I know it, I.
It is some meteor that the sun exhales,
To be to thee this night a torchbearer,

And light thee on thy way to Mantua.   15
Therefore stay yet, thou need'st not to be gone.

ROMEO

Let me be ta'en, let me be put to death;
I am content, so thou wilt have it so.
I'll say yon gray is not the morning's eye,
'Tis but the pale reflex of Cynthia's brow.   20
Nor that is not the lark whose notes do beat
The vaulty heaven so high above our heads;
I have more care to stay than will to go.
Come death, and welcome, Juliet wills it so.
How is't my soul? Let's talk; it is not day.   25

JULIET

It is, it is, hie hence, be gone, away!
It is the lark that sings so out of tune,
Straining harsh discords, and unpleasing sharps.
Some say the lark makes sweet division;
This doth not so, for she divideth us.   30
Some say the lark and loathed toad change eyes,
O now I would they had changed voices too,
Since arm from arm that voice doth us affray,
Hunting thee hence with hunt's-up to the day.
O now be gone; more light and light it grows.   35

ROMEO

More light and light, more dark and dark our woes.
                                        [Enter Nurse.]

NURSE

Madam.

JULIET

Nurse.

NURSE

Your lady mother is coming to your chamber.
The day is broke, be wary, look about.   [Exit.]   40

JULIET

Then window let day in, and let life out.

ROMEO

Farewell, farewell. One kiss, and I'll descend.
                            [Goes down by the ladder.]

JULIET

Art thou gone so, love, lord, ay husband, friend?
I must hear from thee every day in the hour,
For in a minute there are many days.   45
O by this count I shall be much in years,
Ere I again behold my Romeo.

ROMEO

Farewell.
I will omit no opportunity
That may convey my greetings, love, to thee.   50

JULIET

O think'st thou we shall ever meet again?

ROMEO

I doubt it not, and all these woes shall serve
For sweet discourses in our times to come.

JULIET

O God, I have an ill-divining soul.
Methinks I see thee now thou art so low,   55
As one dead in the bottom of a tomb.
Either my eyesight fails, or thou lookest pale.

ROMEO

And trust me love, in my eye so do you.
Dry sorrow drinks our blood. Adieu, adieu.

                                                        [Exit.]

JULIET

O fortune, fortune, all men call thee fickle;   60
If thou art fickle, what dost thou with him
That is renowned for faith? Be fickle, fortune;
For then I hope thou wilt not keep him long,
But send him back.

LADY CAPULET [within]
                    Ho daughter, are you up?   65

JULIET

Who is't that calls? It is my lady mother.
Is she not down so late, or up so early?
What unaccustomed cause procures her hither?

                                        [Enter Lady Capulet.]

LADY CAPULET

Why how now Juliet?

JULIET

Madam I am not well.

LADY CAPULET

Evermore weeping for your cousin's death?   70
What, wilt thou wash him from his grave with tears?
An if thou couldst, thou couldst not make him live.
Therefore have done; some grief shows much of love,
But much of grief shows still some want of wit.

JULIET

Yet let me weep for such a feeling loss.   75

LADY CAPULET

So shall you feel the loss, but not the friend
Which you weep for.

JULIET

Feeling so the loss,
I cannot choose but ever weep the friend.

LADY CAPULET

Well girl, thou weep'st not so much for his death,
As that the villain lives which slaughtered him.   80

JULIET

What villain madam?

LADY CAPULET

That same villain Romeo.

JULIET [aside]

Villain and he be many miles asunder.—
God pardon him; I do with all my heart.
And yet no man like he doth grieve my heart.

LADY CAPULET

That is because the traitor murderer lives.   85

JULIET

Ay madam, from the reach of these my hands.
Would none but I might venge my cousin's death.

LADY CAPULET

We will have vengeance for it, fear thou not,
Then weep no more. I'll send to one in Mantua,
Where that same banished runagate doth live,   90
Shall give him such an unaccustomed dram,

That he shall soon keep Tybalt company.
And then I hope thou wilt be satisfied.
          JULIET
Indeed I never shall be satisfied
With Romeo, till I behold him——dead——   95
Is my poor heart so for a kinsman vexed.
Madam, if you could find out but a man
To bear a poison, I would temper it,
That Romeo should upon receipt thereof
Soon sleep in quiet. O how my heart abhors   100
To hear him named——and cannot come to him——
To wreak the love I bore my cousin
Upon his body that hath slaughtered him.
          LADY CAPULET
Find thou the means, and I'll find such a man.
But now I'll tell thee joyful tidings girl.   105
          JULIET
And joy comes well in such a needy time.
What are they, beseech your ladyship?
          LADY CAPULET
Well, well, thou hast a careful father child,
One who to put thee from thy heaviness
Hath sorted out a sudden day of joy,   110
That thou expects not, nor I looked not for.
          JULIET
Madam, in happy time, what day is that?
          LADY CAPULET
Marry my child, early next Thursday morn,
The gallant, young, and noble gentleman,
The County Paris, at Saint Peter's Church,   115
Shall happily make thee there a joyful bride.
          JULIET
Now by Saint Peter's Church, and Peter too,
He shall not make me there a joyful bride.
I wonder at this haste, that I must wed
Ere he that should be husband comes to woo.   120
I pray you tell my lord and father, madam,
I will not marry yet, and when I do, I swear
It shall be Romeo, whom you know I hate,

Rather than Paris. These are news indeed.

LADY CAPULET

Here comes your father, tell him so yourself;   125
And see how he will take it at your hands.

[*Enter Capulet and Nurse.*]

CAPULET

When the sun sets, the earth doth drizzle dew;
But for the sunset of my brother's son
It rains downright.
How now, a conduit, girl? What, still in tears?   130
Evermore showering? In one little body
Thou counterfeits a bark, a sea, a wind.
For still thy eyes, which I may call the sea,
Do ebb and flow with tears; the bark thy body is,
Sailing in this salt flood; the winds, thy sighs,   135
Who, raging with thy tears, and they with them,
Without a sudden calm, will overset
Thy tempest-tossed body. How now wife,
Have you delivered to her our decree?

LADY CAPULET

Ay sir, but she will none, she gives you thanks.   140
I would the fool were married to her grave.

CAPULET

Soft, take me with you, take me with you wife.
How will she none? Doth she not give us thanks?
Is she not proud? Doth she not count her blessed,
Unworthy as she is, that we have wrought   145
So worthy a gentleman to be her bridegroom?

JULIET

Not proud you have, but thankful that you have.
Proud can I never be of what I hate,
But thankful even for hate, that is meant love.

CAPULET

How, how, how, how, chop-logic, what is this?   150
Proud, and, I thank you, and, I thank you not;
And yet, not proud—mistress minion you,
Thank me no thankings, nor proud me no prouds,
But fettle your fine joints 'gainst Thursday next,
To go with Paris to Saint Peter's Church;   155
Or I will drag thee on a hurdle thither.

Out you green-sickness carrion, out you baggage,
You tallow-face!

    LADY CAPULET

               Fie, fie, what, are you mad?

    JULIET

Good father, I beseech you on my knees,
Hear me with patience, but to speak a word.   160

    CAPULET

Hang thee young baggage, disobedient wretch!
I tell thee what, get thee to church a Thursday,
Or never after look me in the face.
Speak not, reply not, do not answer me.
My fingers itch. Wife, we scarce thought us blessed, 165
That God had lent us but this only child;
But now I see this one is one too much,
And that we have a curse in having her.
Out on her, hilding!

    NURSE

             God in heaven bless her.
You are to blame my lord to rate her so.   170

    CAPULET

And why, my lady wisdom? Hold your tongue.
Good Prudence, smatter with your gossips, go.

    NURSE

I speak no treason.

    CAPULET

          O God ye god-den.

    NURSE

May not one speak?

    CAPULET

          Peace you mumbling fool.
Utter your gravity o'er a gossip's bowl,   175
For here we need it not.

    LADY CAPULET

            You are too hot.

    CAPULET

God's bread, it makes me mad.
Day, night, hour; tide, time; work, play;
Alone, in company; still my care hath been
To have her matched; and having now provided   180

A gentleman of princely parentage,
Of fair demesnes, youthful and nobly trained,
Stuffed as they say with honourable parts,
Proportioned as one's thought would wish a man—
And then to have a wretched puling fool,   185
A whining mammet, in her fortune's tender,
To answer, I'll not wed, I cannot love,
I am too young, I pray you pardon me—
But an you will not wed, I'll pardon you.
Graze where you will, you shall not house with me.   190
Look to't, think on't, I do not use to jest.
Thursday is near, lay hand on heart, advise.
An you be mine, I'll give you to my friend;
An you be not, hang, beg, starve, die in the streets,
For by my soul, I'll ne'er acknowledge thee,   195
Nor what is mine shall never do thee good.
Trust to't, bethink you. I'll not be forsworn.

                                              [*Exit.*]

JULIET
Is there no pity sitting in the clouds,
That sees into the bottom of my grief?
O sweet my mother cast me not away.   200
Delay this marriage for a month, a week,
Or if you do not, make the bridal bed
In that dim monument where Tybalt lies.

LADY CAPULET
Talk not to me, for I'll not speak a word.
Do as thou wilt, for I have done with thee.   205

                                              [*Exit.*]

JULIET
O God! O nurse, how shall this be prevented?
My husband is on earth, my faith in heaven;
How shall that faith return again to earth,
Unless that husband send it me from heaven,
By leaving earth? Comfort me, counsel me.   210
Alack, alack, that heaven should practise stratagems
Upon so soft a subject as myself.
What sayst thou, hast thou not a word of joy?
Some comfort, nurse.

NURSE

                   Faith here it is. Romeo
Is banished; and all the world to nothing,   215
That he dares ne'er come back to challenge you;
Or if he do, it needs must be by stealth.
Then since the case so stands as now it doth,
I think it best you married with the county.
O he's a lovely gentleman.   220
Romeo's a dishclout to him; an eagle, madam,
Hath not so green, so quick, so fair an eye
As Paris hath. Beshrew my very heart,
I think you are happy in this second match,
For it excels your first; or if it did not,   225
Your first is dead, or 'twere as good he were,
As living here, and you no use of him.

JULIET

Speak'st thou from thy heart?

NURSE

And from my soul too, else beshrew them both.

JULIET

Amen.

NURSE

What?

JULIET

Well thou hast comforted me marvellous much.   230
Go in, and tell my lady I am gone,
Having displeased my father, to Laurence' cell,
To make confession, and to be absolved.

NURSE

Marry I will, and this is wisely done.   [*Exit.*]

JULIET

Ancient damnation, o most wicked fiend!   235
Is it more sin to wish me thus forsworn,
Or to dispraise my lord with that same tongue
Which she hath praised him with above compare
So many thousand times? Go counsellor;
Thou and my bosom henceforth shall be twain.   240
I'll to the friar to know his remedy.
If all else fail, myself have power to die.   [*Exit.*]

ACT IV

SCENE ONE.

Verona. Friar Laurence's cell.
Enter Friar Laurence and Paris.

FRIAR LAURENCE
On Thursday sir? The time is very short.
PARIS
My father Capulet will have it so,
And I am nothing slow to slack his haste.
FRIAR LAURENCE
You say you do not know the lady's mind.
Uneven is the course, I like it not.   5
PARIS
Immoderately she weeps for Tybalt's death,
And therefore have I little talked of love,
For Venus smiles not in a house of tears.
Now sir, her father counts it dangerous
That she do give her sorrow so much sway;   10
And in his wisdom hastes our marriage,
To stop the inundation of her tears;
Which too much minded by herself alone,
May be put from her by society.
Now do you know the reason of this haste.   15
FRIAR LAURENCE [*aside*]
I would I knew not why it should be slowed.
                                    [*Enter Juliet.*]
Look sir, here comes the lady toward my cell.
PARIS
Happily met, my lady and my wife.

JULIET

That may be sir, when I may be a wife.

PARIS

That may be, must be, love, on Thursday next.   20

JULIET

What must be shall be.

FRIAR LAURENCE

                That's a certain text.

PARIS

Come you to make confession to this father?

JULIET

To answer that, I should confess to you.

PARIS

Do not deny to him that you love me.

JULIET

I will confess to you that I love him.   25

PARIS

So will ye, I am sure, that you love me.

JULIET

If I do so, it will be of more price,
Being spoke behind your back, than to your face.

PARIS

Pour soul, thy face is much abused with tears.

JULIET

The tears have got small victory by that,   30
For it was bad enough before their spite.

PARIS

Thou wrong'st it more than tears with that report.

JULIET

That is no slander sir, which is a truth,
And what I spake, I spake it to my face.

PARIS

Thy face is mine, and thou hast slandered it.   35

JULIET

It may be so, for it is not mine own.
Are you at leisure, holy father, now,
Or shall I come to you at evening mass?

FRIAR LAURENCE

My leisure serves me pensive daughter now.
My lord, we must entreat the time alone.   40

PARIS

God shield I should disturb devotion.
Juliet, on Thursday early will I rouse ye.
Till then adieu, and keep this holy kiss.   *[Exit.]*

JULIET

O shut the door, and when thou hast done so,
Come weep with me, past hope, past cure, past help.   45

FRIAR LAURENCE

O Juliet I already know thy grief,
It strains me past the compass of my wits.
I hear thou must, and nothing may prorogue it,
On Thursday next be married to this county.

JULIET

Tell me not friar, that thou hearest of this,   50
Unless thou tell me how I may prevent it.
If in thy wisdom thou canst give no help,
Do thou but call my resolution wise,
And with this knife I'll help it presently.
God joined my heart and Romeo's, thou our hands;   55
And ere this hand, by thee to Romeo's sealed,
Shall be the label to another deed,
Or my true heart with treacherous revolt
Turn to another, this shall slay them both.
Therefore out of thy long-experienced time,   60
Give me some present counsel, or behold
'Twixt my extremes and me this bloody knife
Shall play the umpire, arbitrating that
Which the commission of thy years and art
Could to no issue of true honour bring.   65
Be not so long to speak; I long to die,
If what thou speak'st speak not of remedy.

FRIAR LAURENCE

Hold daughter, I do spy a kind of hope,
Which craves as desperate an execution,
As that is desperate which we would prevent.   70
If rather than to marry County Paris
Thou hast the strength of will to slay thyself,
Then is it likely thou wilt undertake
A thing like death to chide away this shame,
That cop'st with death himself to 'scape from it;   75

And if thou darest, I'll give thee remedy.
          JULIET
O bid me leap, rather than marry Paris,
From off the battlements of any tower,
Or walk in thievish ways, or bid me lurk
Where serpents are; chain me with roaring bears,   80
Or hide me nightly in a charnel house,
O'er-covered quite with dead men's rattling bones,
With reeky shanks and yellow chapless skulls.
Or bid me go into a new-made grave,
And hide me with a dead man in his shroud,   85
Things that to hear them told have made me tremble;
And I will do it without fear or doubt,
To live an unstained wife to my sweet love.
          FRIAR LAURENCE
Hold then, go home, be merry, give consent
To marry Paris. Wednesday is to-morrow;   90
To-morrow night look that thou lie alone,
Let not thy nurse lie with thee in thy chamber.
Take thou this vial, being then in bed,
And this distilling liquor drink thou off,
When presently through all thy veins shall run   95
A cold and drowsy humour; for no pulse
Shall keep his native progress, but surcease;
No warmth, no breath, shall testify thou livest,
The roses in thy lips and cheeks shall fade
To waned ashes, thy eyes' windows fall,   100
Like death, when he shuts up the day of life.
Each part deprived of supple government,
Shall stiff and stark and cold appear like death,
And in this borrowed likeness of shrunk death
Thou shalt continue two and forty hours,   105
And then awake as from a pleasant sleep.
Now when the bridegroom in the morning comes
To rouse thee from thy bed, there art thou dead;
Then as the manner of our country is,
In thy best robes, uncovered, on the bier,   110
Thou shalt be borne to that same ancient vault,
Where all the kindred of the Capulets lie.
In the mean time, against thou shalt awake,

Shall Romeo by my letters know our drift,
And hither shall he come, and he and I   115
Will watch thy waking, and that very night
Shall Romeo bear thee hence to Mantua.
And this shall free thee from this present shame,
If no inconstant toy, nor womanish fear,
Abate thy valour in the acting it.   120

      JULIET
Give me, give me, o tell not me of fear.

      FRIAR LAURENCE
Hold. Get you gone, be strong and prosperous
In this resolve; I'll send a friar with speed
To Mantua, with my letters to thy lord.

      JULIET
Love give me strength, and strength shall help afford.   125
Farewell dear father.   [Exeunt.]

      SCENE TWO.

      Verona. A hall in Capulet's house.
      Enter Capulet, Lady Capulet,
      Nurse, and Servants.

      CAPULET
So many guests invite as here are writ.
            [Exit First Servant.]
Sirrah, go hire me twenty cunning cooks.

      SECOND SERVANT
You shall have none ill sir, for I'll try if they can lick
their fingers.

      CAPULET
How canst thou try them so?   5

      SECOND SERVANT
Marry sir, 'tis an ill cook that cannot lick his own

fingers; therefore he that cannot lick his fingers goes
not with me.

CAPULET

Go, be gone.   *[Exit Second Servant.]*
We shall be much unfurnished for this time.   10
What, is my daughter gone to Friar Laurence?

NURSE

Ay forsooth.

CAPULET

Well, he may chance to do some good on her;
A peevish self-willed harlotry it is.

[Enter Juliet.]

NURSE

See where she comes from shrift with merry look.   15

CAPULET

How now my headstrong, where have you been
  gadding?

JULIET

Where I have learned me to repent the sin
Of disobedient opposition
To you and your behests, and am enjoined
By holy Laurence to fall prostrate here,   20
And beg your pardon. *[Kneels.]* Pardon I beseech you,
Henceforward I am ever ruled by you.

CAPULET

Send for the county, go tell him of this.
I'll have this knot knit up to-morrow morning.

JULIET

I met the youthful lord at Laurence' cell,   25
And gave him what becomed love I might,
Not stepping o'er the bounds of modesty.

CAPULET

Why I am glad on't; this is well. Stand up.
This is as't should be. Let me see the county.
Ay marry go I say, and fetch him hither.   30
Now afore God, this reverend holy friar,
All our whole city is much bound to him.

JULIET

Nurse, will you go with me into my closet,

To help me sort such needful ornaments
As you think fit to furnish me to-morrow?   35

LADY CAPULET

No, not till Thursday, there is time enough.

CAPULET

Go nurse, go with her; we'll to church to-morrow.
                              [*Exeunt Juliet and Nurse.*]

LADY CAPULET

We shall be short in our provision;
'Tis now near night.

CAPULET
                              Tush, I will stir about,
And all things shall be well, I warrant thee wife.   40
Go thou to Juliet, help to deck up her;
I'll not to bed to-night, let me alone.
I'll play the housewife for this once. What ho!
They are all forth. Well, I will walk myself
To County Paris, to prepare up him   45
Against to-morrow. My heart is wondrous light,
Since this same wayward girl is so reclaimed.
                                        [*Exeunt.*]

SCENE THREE.

Verona. Juliet's chamber.
Enter Juliet and Nurse.

JULIET

Ay, those attires are best; but gentle nurse,
I pray thee leave me to myself to-night.
For I have need of many orisons,
To move the heavens to smile upon my state,
Which well thou knowest is cross and full of sin.   5
                              [*Enter Lady Capulet.*]

LADY CAPULET
What, are you busy, ho? Need you my help?

JULIET
No madam, we have culled such necessaries
As are behoveful for our state to-morrow.
So please you, let me now be left alone,
And let the nurse this night sit up with you;   10
For I am sure you have your hands full all,
In this so sudden business.

LADY CAPULET
                              Good night.
Get thee to bed and rest, for thou hast need.
                    [*Exeunt Lady Capulet and Nurse.*]

JULIET
Farewell. God knows when we shall meet again.
I have a faint cold fear thrills through my veins   15
That almost freezes up the heat of life.
I'll call them back again to comfort me.
Nurse! What should she do here?
My dismal scene I needs must act alone.
Come vial.   20
What if this mixture do not work at all?
Shall I be married then to-morrow morning?
No, no, this shall forbid it. Lie thou there.
                              [*Lays down her dagger.*]
What if it be a poison which the friar
Subtly hath ministered to have me dead,   25
Lest in this marriage he should be dishonoured,
Because he married me before to Romeo?
I fear it is, and yet methinks it should not,
For he hath still been tried a holy man.
How if when I am laid into the tomb,   30
I wake before the time that Romeo
Come to redeem me—there's a fearful point.
Shall I not then be stifled in the vault,
To whose foul mouth no healthsome air breathes in,
And there die strangled ere my Romeo comes?   35
Or if I live, is it not very like,
The horrible conceit of death and night,

Together with the terror of the place—
As in a vault, an ancient receptacle,
Where for this many hundred years the bones   40
Of all my buried ancestors are packed,
Where bloody Tybalt yet but green in earth
Lies festering in his shroud, where as they say,
At some hours in the night spirits resort—
Alack, alack, is it not like that I,   45
So early waking—what with loathsome smells,
And shrieks like mandrakes torn out of the earth,
That living mortals hearing them run mad—
O if I wake, shall I not be distraught,
Environed with all these hideous fears,   50
And madly play with my forefathers' joints,
And pluck the mangled Tybalt from his shroud,
And in this rage, with some great kinsman's bone,
As with a club, dash out my desperate brains?
O look, methinks I see my cousin's ghost,   55
Seeking out Romeo that did spit his body
Upon a rapier's point—stay Tybalt, stay!
Romeo! Romeo! Romeo! I drink to thee.

> [*Drinks and falls on her bed. The curtains close.*]

SCENE FOUR.

Verona. A hall in Capulet's house.
Enter Lady Capulet and Nurse.

LADY CAPULET
Hold, take these keys, and fetch more spices, nurse.
    NURSE
They call for dates and quinces in the pastry.

> [*Enter Capulet.*]

    CAPULET
Come, stir, stir, stir, the second cock hath crowed,
The curfew bell hath rung, 'tis three a clock.

Look to the baked meats, good Angelica,   5
Spare not for cost.
      NURSE
                 Go you cot-quean, go,
Get you to bed; faith you'll be sick to-morrow
For this night's watching.
      CAPULET
No, not a whit; what, I have watched ere now
All night for lesser cause, and ne'er been sick.   10
      LADY CAPULET
Ay you have been a mouse-hunt in your time,
But I will watch you from such watching now.
           [Exeunt Lady Capulet and Nurse.]
      CAPULET
A jealous-hood, a jealous-hood.
      [Enter Servants with spits, and logs, and
      baskets.]
                    Now fellow,
What is there?
      FIRST SERVANT
Things for the cook, sir, but I know not what.
      CAPULET
Make haste, make haste. *[Exit First Servant.]* Sirrah
   fetch drier logs.   15
Call Peter, he will show thee where they are.
      SECOND SERVANT
I have a head sir, that will find out logs,
And never trouble Peter for the matter.
      CAPULET
Mass and well said, a merry whoreson, ha!
Thou shall be logger-head. *[Exeunt Servants.]* God
   Father, 'tis day.   20
The county will be here with music straight,
For so he said he would. *[Music.]* I hear him near.
Nurse! Wife! What ho! What, nurse I say!
                   [Enter Nurse.]
Go waken Juliet, go and trim her up.
I'll go and chat with Paris. Hie, make haste,   25
Make haste; the bridegroom he is come already.
Make haste I say.   *[Exeunt.]*

SCENE FIVE.

Verona. Juliet's chamber. Enter Nurse.

NURSE [*draws curtains*]
Mistress! What, mistress! Juliet! Fast, I warrant her.
  She—
Why lamb, why lady—fie you slug-a-bed!
Why love I say! Madam! Sweetheart! Why bride!
What, not a word? You take your pennyworths now.
Sleep for a week; for the next night I warrant   5
The County Paris hath set up his rest
That you shall rest but little, God forgive me.
Marry, and amen. How sound is she asleep!
I needs must wake her. Madam, madam, madam!
Ay, let the county take you in your bed,   10
He'll fright you up i' faith. Will it not be?
What, dressed, and in your clothes, and down again?
I must needs wake you. Lady, lady, lady!
Alas, alas, help, help, my lady's dead!
O, weladay that ever I was born!   15
Some aqua-vitae ho! My lord! My lady!
                          [*Enter Lady Capulet.*]

LADY CAPULET
What noise is here?

NURSE
              O lamentable day.

LADY CAPULET
What is the matter?

NURSE
              Look, look, o heavy day.

LADY CAPULET
O me, o me, my child, my only life.

Revive, look up, or I will die with thee.   20
Help, help! Call help.

> [*Enter Capulet.*]

CAPULET
For shame, bring Juliet forth; her lord is come.
NURSE
She's dead, deceased, she's dead, alack the day!
LADY CAPULET
Alack the day, she's dead, she's dead, she's dead!
CAPULET
Ha! Let me see her. Out alas she's cold,   25
Her blood is settled, and her joints are stiff.
Life and these lips have long been separated.
Death lies on her like an untimely frost
Upon the sweetest flower of all the field.
NURSE
O lamentable day.
LADY CAPULET
          O woeful time.   30
CAPULET
Death that hath ta'en her hence to make me wail,
Ties up my tongue, and will not let me speak.
> [*Enter Friar Laurence and Paris, with
> Catling, Rebeck, and Soundpost.*]
FRIAR LAURENCE
Come, is the bride ready to go to church?
CAPULET
Ready to go, but never to return.
O son, the night before thy wedding-day   35
Hath Death lain with thy wife; there she lies,
Flower as she was, deflowered by him.
Death is my son-in-law, Death is my heir,
My daughter he hath wedded. I will die,
And leave him all; life, living, all is Death's.   40
PARIS
Have I thought, love, to see this morning's face,
And doth it give me such a sight as this?
LADY CAPULET
Accursed, unhappy, wretched, hateful day,

Most miserable hour that e'er time saw
In lasting labour of his pilgrimage!   45
But one, poor one, one poor and loving child,
But one thing to rejoice and solace in,
And cruel Death hath catched it from my sight.

NURSE

O woe, o woeful, woeful, woeful day,
Most lamentable day, most woeful day   50
That ever, ever, I did yet behold!
O day, o day, o day, o hateful day,
Never was seen so black a day as this.
O woeful day, o woeful day!

PARIS

Beguiled, divorced, wronged, spited, slain,   55
Most detestable Death, by thee beguiled,
By cruel, cruel thee, quite overthrown!
O life, o life; not life, but love in death.

CAPULET

Despised, distressed, hated, martyred, killed!
Uncomfortable time, why cam'st thou now   60
To murder, murder, our solemnity?
O child, o child, my soul and not my child,
Dead art thou, alack my child is dead,
And with my child my joys are buried.

FRIAR LAURENCE

Peace ho for shame! Confusion's cure lives not   65
In these confusions. Heaven and yourself
Had part in this fair maid, now heaven hath all,
And all the better is it for the maid.
Your part in her you could not keep from death,
But heaven keeps his part in eternal life.   70
The most you sought was her promotion,
For 'twas your heaven she should be advanced
And weep ye now, seeing she is advanced
Above the clouds, as high as heaven itself?
O in this love, you love your child so ill,   75
That you run mad, seeing that she is well.
She's not well married that lives married long,
But she's best married that dies married young.
Dry up your tears, and stick your rosemary

On this fair corse; and as the custom is,   80
All in her best array bear her to church.
For though fond nature bids us all lament,
Yet nature's tears are reason's merriment.
        CAPULET
All things that we ordained festival
Turn from their office to black funeral;   85
Our instruments to melancholy bells,
Our wedding cheer to a sad burial feast;
Our solemn hymns to sullen dirges change,
Our bridal flowers serve for a buried corse,
And all things change them to the contrary.   90
        FRIAR LAURENCE
Sir, go you in, and madam, go with him,
And go Sir Paris; every one prepare
To follow this fair corse unto her grave.
The heavens do lour upon you for some ill;
Move them no more, by crossing their high will.   95
        [Exeunt. Nurse, Catling, Rebeck, and Sound-
        post remain.]
        CATLING
Faith we may put up our pipes and be gone.
        NURSE
Honest good fellows, ah put up, put up,
For well you know this is a pitiful case.   [Exit.]
        CATLING
Ay by my troth, the case may be amended.   100
                         [Enter Peter.]
        PETER
Musicians, o musicians, heart's ease, heart's ease.
O an you will have me live, play heart's ease.
        CATLING
Why heart's ease?   105
        PETER
O musicians, because my heart itself plays, my heart
is full. O play me some merry dump to comfort me.
        CATLING
Not a dump we, 'tis no time to play now.   110
        PETER
You will not then?

CATLING

No.

PETER

I will then give it you soundly.

CATLING

What will you give us?

PETER

No money on my faith, but the gleek. I will give 115
you the minstrel.

CATLING

Then will I give you the serving-creature.

PETER

Then will I lay the serving-creature's dagger on your
pate. I will carry no crochets. I'll re you, I'll fa you, 120
do you note me?

CATLING

And you re us and fa us, you note us.

REBECK

Pray you, put up your dagger, and put out your wit.

PETER

Then have at you with my wit. I will dry-beat you 125
with an iron wit, and put up my iron dagger. Answer
me like men.   [Sings.]

    When griping grief the heart doth wound,
    And doleful dumps the mind oppress,
    Then music with her silver sound—   130
why silver sound, why music with her silver sound?
What say you Simon Catling?

CATLING

Marry sir, because silver hath a sweet sound.

PETER

Pretty. What say you Hugh Rebeck?   135

REBECK

I say, silver sound, because musicians sound for silver.

PETER

Pretty too. What say you James Soundpost?

SOUNDPOST

Faith I know not what to say.   140

PETER

O I cry you mercy; you are the singer. I will say for

you, it is music with her silver sound, because musicians have no gold for sounding.   [*Sings.*]

    Then music with her silver sound   145
    With speedy help doth lend redress.   [*Exit.*]

    CATLING

What a pestilent knave is this same!

    REBECK

Hang him, Jack! Come we'll in here, tarry for the
mourners, and stay dinner.   [*Exeunt.*]   150

ACT V

SCENE ONE.

Mantua. A street. Enter Romeo.

ROMEO

If I may trust the flattering truth of sleep,
My dreams presage some joyful news at hand.
My bosom's lord sits lightly in his throne;
And all this day an unaccustomed spirit
Lifts me above the ground with cheerful thoughts.   5
I dreamt my lady came and found me dead—
Strange dream that gives a dead man leave to think——
And breathed such life with kisses in my lips,
That I revived and was an emperor.
Ah me, how sweet is love itself possessed,   10
When but love's shadows are so rich in joy.

                    [Enter Balthasar.]

News from Verona. How now Balthasar,
Dost thou not bring me letters from the friar?
How doth my lady? Is my father well?
How fares my Juliet? That I ask again,   15
For nothing can be ill if she be well.

BALTHASAR

Then she is well and nothing can be ill.
Her body sleeps in Capels' monument,
And her immortal part with angels lives.
I saw her laid low in her kindred's vault,   20
And presently took post to tell it you.
O pardon me for bringing these ill news,
Since you did leave it for my office sir.

ROMEO

Is it even so? Then I defy you, stars.
Thou knowest my lodging, get me ink and paper,   25
And hire post-horses; I will hence to-night.

BALTHASAR

I do beseech you sir, have patience.
Your looks are pale and wild, and do import
Some misadventure.

ROMEO

          Tush, thou art deceived.
Leave me, and do the thing I bid thee do.   30
Hast thou no letters to me from the friar?

BALTHASAR

No my good lord.

ROMEO

          No matter. Get thee gone,
And hire those horses; I'll be with thee straight.
                    [Exit Balthasar.]
Well Juliet, I will lie with thee to-night.
Let's see for means. O mischief, thou art swift   35
To enter in the thoughts of desperate men.
I do remember an apothecary—
And hereabouts 'a dwells—which late I noted,
In tattered weeds, with overwhelming brows,
Culling of simples; meagre were his looks,   40
Sharp misery had worn him to the bones;
And in his needy shop a tortoise hung,
An alligator stuffed, and other skins
Of ill-shaped fishes, and about his shelves
A beggarly account of empty boxes,   45
Green earthen pots, bladders, and musty seeds,
Remnants of packthread, and old cakes of roses,
Were thinly scattered, to make up a show.
Noting this penury, to myself I said,
An if a man did need a poison now,   50
Whose sale is present death in Mantua,
Here lives a caitiff wretch would sell it him.
O this same thought did but forerun my need,
And this same needy man must sell it me.

As I remember, this should be the house.   55
Being holiday, the beggar's shop is shut.
What ho apothecary!

> *[Enter Apothecary.]*

APOTHECARY
                    Who calls so loud?
ROMEO
Come hither man. I see that thou art poor.
Hold, there is forty ducats, let me have
A dram of poison, such soon-speeding gear   60
As will disperse itself through all the veins,
That the life-weary taker may fall dead,
And that the trunk may be discharged of breath,
As violently as hasty powder fired
Doth hurry from the fatal cannon's womb.   65
APOTHECARY
Such mortal drugs I have, but Mantua's law
Is death to any he that utters them.
ROMEO
Art thou so bare and full of wretchedness,
And fearest to die? Famine is in thy cheeks,
Need and oppression starveth in thy eyes,   70
Contempt and beggary hangs upon thy back.
The world is not thy friend, nor the world's law,
The world affords no law to make thee rich;
Then be not poor, but break it, and take this.
APOTHECARY
My poverty, but not my will consents.   75
ROMEO
I pay thy poverty and not thy will.
APOTHECARY
Put this in any liquid thing you will
And drink it off, and if you had the strength
Of twenty men, it would dispatch you straight.
ROMEO
There is thy gold, worse poison to men's souls,   80
Doing more murder in this loathsome world,
Than these poor compounds that thou mayst not sell.
I sell thee poison, thou hast sold me none.

Farewell, buy food, and get thyself in flesh.
Come cordial, and not poison, go with me.   85
To Juliet's grave, for there must I use thee.

[Exeunt.]

SCENE TWO.

Verona. Friar Laurence's cell.
Enter Friar John.

FRIAR JOHN
Holy Franciscan friar, brother, ho!

[Enter Friar Laurence.]

FRIAR LAURENCE
This same should be the voice of Friar John.
Welcome from Mantua. What says Romeo?
Or if his mind be writ, give me his letter.

FRIAR JOHN
Going to find a barefoot brother out,   5
One of our order, to associate me,
Here in this city visiting the sick,
And finding him, the searchers of the town,
Suspecting that we both were in a house
Where the infectious pestilence did reign,   10
Sealed up the doors, and would not let us forth,
So that my speed to Mantua there was stayed.

FRIAR LAURENCE
Who bare my letter then to Romeo?

FRIAR JOHN
I could not send it, here it is again—
Nor get a messenger to bring it thee,   15
So fearful were they of infection.

FRIAR LAURENCE
Unhappy fortune! By my brotherhood,
The letter was not nice, but full of charge
Of dear import; and the neglecting it

May do much danger. Friar John, go hence,   20
Get me an iron crow and bring it straight
Unto my cell.

    FRIAR JOHN

Brother I'll go and bring it thee.   [*Exit.*]

    FRIAR LAURENCE

Now must I to the monument alone;
Within this three hours will fair Juliet wake.
She will beshrew me much that Romeo   25
Hath had no notice of these accidents.
But I will write again to Mantua,
And keep her at my cell till Romeo come—
Poor living corse closed in a dead man's tomb.

                                    [*Exit.*]

SCENE THREE.

Verona. A churchyard; the monument of the Capulets. Enter Paris and Page.

    PARIS

Give me thy torch boy; hence, and stand aloof.
Yet put it out, for I would not be seen.
Under yond yew trees lay thee all along,
Holding thy ear close to the hollow ground;
So shall no foot upon the churchyard tread—   5
Being loose, unfirm with digging up of graves—
But thou shalt hear it; whistle then to me,
As signal that thou hearest something approach.
Give me those flowers. Do as I bid thee, go.

    PAGE

I am almost afraid to stand alone,   10
Here in the churchyard, yet I will adventure.

                                 [*Retires.*]

    PARIS

Sweet flower, with flowers thy bridal bed I strew.

O woe, thy canopy is dust and stones.
Which with sweet water nightly I will dew,
Or wanting that, with tears distilled by moans.   15
The obsequies that I for thee will keep,
Nightly shall be to strew thy grave and weep.
                                    [*Page whistles.*]
The boy gives warning something doth approach.
What cursed foot wanders this way to-night,
To cross my obsequies and true love's rite?   20
What, with a torch! Muffle me night awhile.
                [*Retires. Enter Romeo and Balthasar.*]
        ROMEO
Give me that mattock and the wrenching iron.
Hold, take this letter; early in the morning
See thou deliver it to my lord and father.
Give me the light. Upon thy life I charge thee,   25
Whate'er thou hearest or seest, stand all aloof,
And do not interrupt me in my course.
Why I descend into this bed of death,
Is partly to behold my lady's face;
But chiefly to take thence from her dead finger   30
A precious ring—a ring that I must use
In dear employment. Therefore hence, be gone.
But if thou, jealous, dost return to pry
In what I farther shall intend to do,
By heaven I will tear thee joint by joint,   35
And strew this hungry churchyard with thy limbs.
The time and my intents are savage-wild,
More fierce and more inexorable far,
Than empty tigers, or the roaring sea.
        BALTHASAR
I will be gone sir, and not trouble you.   40
        ROMEO
So shalt thou show me friendship. Take thou that.
Live and be prosperous, and farewell good fellow.
        BALTHASAR [*aside*]
For all this same, I'll hide me hereabout.
His looks I fear, and his intents I doubt.   [*Retires.*]
        ROMEO
Thou detestable maw, thou womb of death,   45

Gorged with the dearest morsel of the earth,
Thus I enforce thy rotten jaws to open,

[*Opens the tomb.*]

And in despite I'll cram thee with more food.

PARIS

This is that banished haughty Montague,
That murdered my love's cousin, with which grief   50
It is supposed that fair creature died,
And here is come to do some villainous shame
To the dead bodies. I will apprehend him.
Stop thy unhallowed toil vile Montague.
Can vengeance be pursued further than death?   55
Condemned villain, I do apprehend thee.
Obey and go with me, for thou must die.

ROMEO

I must indeed, and therefore came I hither.
Good gentle youth, tempt not a desperate man;
Fly hence and leave me. Think upon these gone,   60
Let them affright thee. I beseech thee youth,
Put not another sin upon my head,
By urging me to fury. O be gone.
By heaven, I love thee better than myself,
For I come hither armed against myself.   65
Stay not, be gone, live, and hereafter say,
A madman's mercy bid thee run away.

PARIS

I do defy thy conjurations,
And apprehend thee for a felon here.

ROMEO

Wilt thou provoke me? Then have at thee boy.   70

[*They fight.*]

PAGE

O lord, they fight, I will go call the watch.   [*Exit.*]

PARIS

O I am slain! If thou be merciful,
Open the tomb, lay me with Juliet.   [*Dies.*]

ROMEO

In faith I will. Let me peruse this face.
Mercutio's kinsman, noble County Paris!   75

What said my man, when my betossed soul
Did not attend him as we rode? I think
He told me Paris should have married Juliet.
Said he not so? Or did I dream it so?
Or am I mad, hearing him talk of Juliet,   80
To think it was so? O give me thy hand,
One writ with me in sour misfortune's book.
I'll bury thee in a triumphant grave.
A grave? O no, a lantern, slaughtered youth.
For here lies Juliet, and her beauty makes   85
This vault a feasting presence full of light.
Death, lie thou there, by a dead man interred.
                              [*Lays Paris in the tomb.*]
How oft when men are at the point of death
Have they been merry, which their keepers call
A lightning before death. O how may I   90
Call this a lightning? O my love, my wife!
Death that hath sucked the honey of thy breath,
Hath had no power yet upon thy beauty.
Thou art not conquered; beauty's ensign yet
Is crimson in thy lips and in thy cheeks,   95
And death's pale flag is not advanced there.
Tybalt, liest thou there in thy bloody sheet?
O what more favour can I do to thee,
Than with that hand that cut thy youth in twain
To sunder his that was thine enemy?   100
Forgive me cousin. Ah dear Juliet,
Why art thou yet so fair? Shall I believe
That unsubstantial Death is amorous,
And that the lean abhorred monster keeps
Thee here in dark to be his paramour?   105
For fear of that, I still will stay with thee,
And never from this palace of dim night*
Depart again. Here, here will I remain,
Depart again, come lie thou in my arm,
Here's to thy health, where'er thou tumblest in.
O true apothecary!

Lines deleted in rewriting:

Thy drugs are quick. Thus with a kiss I die.
With worms that are thy chamber-maids. O here
Will I set up my everlasting rest;   110
And shake the yoke of inauspicious stars
From this world-wearied flesh. Eyes look your last.
Arms, take your last embrace. And lips, o you
The doors of breath, seal with a righteous kiss
A dateless bargain to engrossing death.   115
Come bitter conduct, come unsavoury guide,
Thou desperate pilot, now at once run on
The dashing rocks thy sea-sick weary bark.
Here's to my love! O true apothecary!
Thy drugs are quick. Thus with a kiss I die.   120

[*Enter Friar Laurence, with lantern, crow, and
spade.*]

FRIAR LAURENCE
Saint Francis be my speed. How oft to-night
Have my old feet stumbled at graves. Who's there?

BALTHASAR
Here's one, a friend, and one that knows you well.

FRIAR LAURENCE
Bliss be upon you. Tell me good my friend,
What torch is yond, that vainly lends his light   125
To grubs and eyeless skulls? As I discern,
It burneth in the Capels' monument.

BALTHASAR
It doth so holy sir, and there's my master,
One that you love.

FRIAR LAURENCE
                Who is it?

BALTHASAR
                            Romeo.

FRIAR LAURENCE
How long hath he been there?

BALTHASAR
                            Full half an hour.   130

FRIAR LAURENCE
Go with me to the vault.

BALTHASAR
                    I dare not sir.

My master knows not but I am gone hence,
And fearfully did menace me with death
If I did stay to look on his intents.

FRIAR LAURENCE
Stay then, I'll go alone. Fear comes upon me.   135
O much I fear some ill unlucky thing.

BALTHASAR
As I did sleep under this yew tree here,
I dreamt my master and another fought,
And that my master slew him.

FRIAR LAURENCE
                                                Romeo!
Alack, alack, what blood is this which stains   140
The stony entrance of this sepulchre?
What mean these masterless and gory swords
To lie discoloured by this place of peace?
                                     [*Enters the tomb.*]
Romeo! O, pale! Who else? What, Paris too?
And steeped in blood? Ah what an unkind hour   145
Is guilty of this lamentable chance!
The lady stirs.

JULIET
O comfortable friar, where is my lord?
I do remember well where I should be,
And there I am. Where is my Romeo? [*Noise within.*]   150

FRIAR LAURENCE
I hear some noise. Lady, come from that nest
Of death, contagion, and unnatural sleep.
A greater power than we can contradict
Hath thwarted our intents. Come, come away.
Thy husband in thy bosom there lies dead;   155
And Paris too. Come I'll dispose of thee
Among a sisterhood of holy nuns.
Stay not to question, for the watch is coming;
Come, go good Juliet, I dare no longer stay.
                                              [*Exit.*]

JULIET
Go get thee hence, for I will not away.   160
What's here? A cup closed in my true love's hand?
Poison I see hath been his timeless end.

O churl, drunk all; and left no friendly drop
To help me after? I will kiss thy lips;
Haply some poison yet doth hang on them,   165
To make me die with a restorative.
Thy lips are warm.

     CHIEF WATCHMAN [*within*]
Lead boy. Which way?

     JULIET
Yea, noise? Then I'll be brief. O happy dagger!
                    [Draws Romeo's dagger.]
This is thy sheath; there rust, and let me die.   170
           [Stabs herself. Enter Watch, with Page.]

     PAGE
This is the place; there where the torch doth burn.

     CHIEF WATCHMAN
The ground is bloody, search about the churchyard.
Go some of you, whoe'er you find attach.
                [Exeunt some of the Watch.]
Pitiful sight! Here lies the county slain,
And Juliet bleeding, warm, and newly dead,   175
Who here hath lain this two days buried.
Go tell the Prince, run to the Capulets,
Raise up the Montagues, some others search.
We see the ground whereon these woes do lie,
But the true ground of all these piteous woes   180
We cannot without circumstance descry.
       [Enter some of the Watch, with Balthasar.]

     SECOND WATCHMAN
Here's Romeo's man, we found him in the churchyard.

     CHIEF WATCHMAN
Hold him in safety, till the Prince come hither.
     [Enter Friar Laurence, and another Watchman.]
     THIRD WATCHMAN
Here is a friar that trembles, sighs, and weeps.
We took this mattock and this spade from him,   185
As he was coming from this churchyard's side.

     CHIEF WATCHMAN
A great suspicion. Stay the friar too.
              [Enter Prince and attendants.]

PRINCE

What misadventure is so early up,
That calls our person from our morning rest?
                    [*Enter Capulet and Lady Capulet.*]

CAPULET

What should it be that is so shrieked abroad?   190

LADY CAPULET

The people in the street cry Romeo,
Some Juliet, and some Paris, and all run
With open outcry toward our monument.

PRINCE

What fear is this which startles in your ears?

CHIEF WATCHMAN

Sovereign, here lies the County Paris slain,   195
And Romeo dead, and Juliet, dead before,
Warm and new killed.

PRINCE

Search, seek, and know how this foul murder comes.

CHIEF WATCHMAN

Here is a friar, and slaughtered Romeo's man,
With instruments upon them, fit to open   200
These dead men's tombs.

CAPULET

O heavens! O wife, look how our daughter bleeds.
This dagger hath mista'en, for lo his house
Is empty on the back of Montague,
And it mis-sheathed in my daughter's bosom.   205

LADY CAPULET

O me, this sight of death is as a bell,
That warns my old age to a sepulchre.

                              [*Enter Montague.*]

PRINCE

Come Montague, for thou art early up,
To see thy son and heir more early down.

MONTAGUE

Alas my liege, my wife is dead to-night;   210
Grief of my son's exile hath stopped her breath.
What further woe conspires against mine age?

PRINCE

Look and thou shalt see.

MONTAGUE
O thou untaught, what manners is in this,
To press before thy father to a grave?   215

PRINCE
Seal up the mouth of outrage for a while,
Till we can clear these ambiguities,
And know their spring, their head, their true descent;
And then will I be general of your woes,
And lead you even to death. Meantime forbear,   220
And let mischance be slave to patience.
Bring forth the parties of suspicion.

FRIAR LAURENCE
I am the greatest, able to do least,
Yet most suspected, as the time and place
Doth make against me, of this direful murder.   225
And here I stand both to impeach and purge
Myself condemned, and myself excused.

PRINCE
Then say at once what thou dost know in this.

FRIAR LAURENCE
I will be brief, for my short date of breath
Is not so long as is a tedious tale.   230
Romeo, there dead, was husband to that Juliet,
And she, there dead, that Romeo's faithful wife.
I married them, and their stolen marriage day
Was Tybalt's doomsday, whose untimely death
Banished the new-made bridegroom from this city;   235
For whom, and not for Tybalt, Juliet pined.
You, to remove that siege of grief from her,
Betrothed, and would have married her perforce,
To County Paris. Then comes she to me,
And with wild looks bid me devise some mean   240
To rid her from this second marriage,
Or in my cell there would she kill herself.
Then gave I her, so tutored by my art,
A sleeping potion; which so took effect
As I intended, for it wrought on her   245
The form of death. Meantime I writ to Romeo,
That he should hither come as this dire night,
To help to take her from her borrowed grave,

Being the time the potion's force should cease.
But he which bore my letter, Friar John,   250
Was stayed by accident, and yesternight
Returned my letter back. Then all alone
At the prefixed hour of her waking,
Came I to take her from her kindred's vault,
Meaning to keep her closely at my cell,   255
Till I conveniently could send to Romeo.
But when I came, some minute ere the time
Of her awakening, here untimely lay
The noble Paris and true Romeo dead.
She wakes, and I entreated her come forth,   260
And bear this work of heaven with patience.
But then a noise did scare me from the tomb,
And she, too desperate, would not go with me,
But as it seems, did violence on herself.
All this I know, and to the marriage   265
Her nurse is privy; and if aught in this
Miscarried by my fault, let my old life
Be sacrificed some hour before his time,
Unto the rigour of severest law.

PRINCE
We still have known thee for a holy man.   270
Where's Romeo's man? What can he say to this?

BALTHASAR
I brought my master news of Juliet's death,
And then in post he came from Mantua,
To this same place, to this same monument.
This letter he early bid me give his father,   275
And threatened me with death, going in the vault,
If I departed not, and left him there.

PRINCE
Give me the letter, I will look on it.
Where is the county's page that raised the watch?
Sirrah, what made your master in this place?   280

PAGE
He came with flowers to strew his lady's grave,
And bid me stand aloof, and so I did.
Anon comes one with light to ope the tomb,
And by and by my master drew on him,

And then I ran away to call the watch.   285
      PRINCE
This letter doth make good the friar's words,
Their course of love, the tidings of her death;
And here he writes, that he did buy poison
Of a poor pothecary, and therewithal
Came to this vault, to die, and lie with Juliet.   290
Where be these enemies? Capulet, Montague,
See what a scourge is laid upon your hate,
That heaven finds means to kill your joys with love.
And I for winking at your discords too
Have lost a brace of kinsmen; all are punished.   295
      CAPULET
O brother Montague, give me thy hand.
This is my daughter's jointure, for no more
Can I demand.
      MONTAGUE
              But I can give thee more,
For I will raise her statue in pure gold,
That while Verona by that name is known,   300
There shall no figure at such rate be set
As that of true and faithful Juliet.
      CAPULET
As rich shall Romeo's by his lady's lie,
Poor sacrifices of our enmity.
      PRINCE
A glooming peace this morning with it brings;   305
The sun, for sorrow, will not show his head.
Go hence, to have more talk of these sad things;
Some shall be pardoned, and some punished.
For never was a story of more woe,
Than this of Juliet and her Romeo.   *[Exeunt.]*   310

WEST SIDE STORY

A MUSICAL
(Based on a conception of Jerome Robbins)
Book by ARTHUR LAURENTS
Music by LEONARD BERNSTEIN
Lyrics by STEPHEN SONDHEIM
Entire production directed and
choreographed by JEROME ROBBINS

WEST SIDE STORY *was first presented by Robert E. Griffith and Harold S. Prince, by arrangement with Roger L. Stevens, at the Winter Garden, New York City, September 26, 1957, with the following cast:*

THE JETS

RIFF, *the leader—Mickey Calin*
TONY, *his friend—Larry Kert*
ACTION—*Eddie Roll*
A-RAB—*Tony Mordente*
BABY JOHN—*David Winters*
SNOWBOY—*Grover Dale*
BIG DEAL—*Martin Charnin*
DIESEL—*Hank Brunjes*
GEE-TAR—*Tommy Abbott*
MOUTHPIECE—*Frank Green*
TIGER—*Lowell Harris*

THEIR GIRLS

GRAZIELLA—*Wilma Curley*
VELMA—*Carole D'Andrea*
MINNIE—*Nanette Rosen*
CLARICE—*Marilyn D'Honau*
PAULINE—*Julie Oser*
ANYBODYS—*Lee Becker*

THE SHARKS

BERNARDO, *the leader—Ken Le Roy*
MARIA, *his sister—Carol Lawrence*
ANITA, *his girl—Chita Rivera*
CHINO, *hs friend—Jamie Sanchez*

PEPE—*George Marcy*
INDIO—*Noel Schwartz*
LUIS—*Al De Sio*
ANXIOUS—*Gene Gavin*
NIBBLES—*Ronnie Lee*
JUANO—*Jay Norman*
TORO—*Erne Castaldo*
MOOSE—*Jack Murray*

THEIR GIRLS

ROSALIA—*Marilyn Cooper*
CONSUELO—*Reri Grist*
TERESITA—*Carmen Guiterrez*
FRANCISCA—*Elizabeth Taylor*
ESTELLA—*Lynn Ross*
MARGARITA—*Liane Plane*

THE ADULTS

DOC—*Art Smith*
SCHRANK—*Arch Johnson*
KRUPKE—*William Bramley*
GLAD HAND—*John Harkins*

Scenic production by Oliver Smith
Costumes designed by Irene Sharaff
Lighting by Jean Rosenthal
Musical direction by Max Goberman
Orchestrations by Leonard Bernstein,
with Sid Ramin *and* Irwin Kostal
Co-choreographer: Peter Gennaro
Production Associate: Sylvia Drulie

SCENE: *The action takes place on the West Side of New York City during the last days of summer.*

ACT ONE

PROLOGUE: THE MONTHS BEFORE

5:00 P.M., *The Street*
5:30 P.M., *A Back Yard*
6:00 P.M., *A Bridal Shop*
10:00 P.M., *The Gym*
11:00 P.M., *A Back Alley*
MIDNIGHT, *The Drugstore*

THE NEXT DAY

5:30 P.M., *The Bridal Shop*
6:00 to 9:00 P.M., *The Neighborhood*
9:00 P.M., *Under the Highway*

ACT TWO

9:15 P.M., *A Bedroom*
10:00 P.M., *Another Alley*
11:30 P.M., *The Bedroom*
11:40 P.M., *The Drugstore*
11:50 P.M., *The Cellar*
MIDNIGHT, *The Street*

MUSICAL NUMBERS

ACT ONE

PROLOGUE, *Danced by Jets and Sharks*

JET SONG, *Riff and Jets*

"SOMETHING'S COMING", *Tony*

THE DANCE AT THE GYM, *Jets and Sharks*

"MARIA", *Tony*

"TONIGHT", *Tony and Maria*

"AMERICA", *Anita, Rosalia, and Shark Girls*

"COOL", *Riff and the Jets*

"ONE HAND, ONE HEART", *Tony and Maria*

"TONIGHT" (Quintet and Chorus), *Company*

THE RUMBLE, *Riff, Bernardo, Jets and Sharks*

ACT TWO

"I FEEL PRETTY", *Maria, Rosalia, Teresita, Francisca*

"SOMEWHERE", *Danced by Company; Sung by Consuelo*

"GEE, OFFICER KRUPKE", *Action, Snowboy, and Jets*

"A BOY LIKE THAT", *Anita and Maria*

"I HAVE A LOVE", *Anita and Maria*

TAUNTING, *Anita and the Jets*

FINALE, *Company*

ACT I

SCENE ONE.

5:00 P.M. *The street.*

A suggestion of city streets and alleyways; a brick wall.

The opening is musical: half-danced, half-mimed, with occasional phrases of dialogue. It is primarily a condensation of the growing rivalry between two teen-age gangs, the Jets and the Sharks, each of which has its own prideful uniform. The boys—sideburned, long-haired—are vital, restless, sardonic; the Sharks are Puerto Ricans, the Jets an anthology of what is called "American."

The action begins with the Jets in possession of the area: owning, enjoying, loving their "home." Their leader is Riff: glowing, driving, intelligent, slightly whacky. His lieutenant is Diesel: big, slow, steady, nice. The youngest member of the gang is Baby John: awed at everything, including that he is a Jet, trying to act the big man. His buddy is A-rab: an explosive little ferret who enjoys everything and understands the seriousness of nothing. The most aggressive is Action: a catlike ball of fury. We will get to know these boys better later, as well as Snowboy: a bespectacled self-styled expert.

The first interruption of the Jets' sunny mood is the sharply punctuated entrance of the leader of the Sharks, Bernardo: handsome, proud, fluid, a chip on his sardonic shoulder. The Jets, by far in the majority, flick him off. He returns with other Sharks: they, too, are flicked off. But the numerical supremacy, the strength of the Jets, is gradually being threatened. The beginnings of warfare are mild at first: a boy being tripped up, or being sandbagged with a

*flour sack or even being spit on——all with overly elaborate
apologies.*

*Finally, A-rab comes across the suddenly deserted area,
pretending to be an airplane. There is no sound as he zooms
along in fancied flight. Then over the wall drops Bernardo.
Another Shark, another and another appear, blocking
A-rab's panicky efforts at escape. They close in, grab him,
pummel him, as a Shark on top of the wall is stationed
as lookout. Finally, Bernardo bends over A-rab and makes
a gesture (piercing his ear); the lookout whistles; Jets tear
on, Sharks tear on, and a free-for-all breaks out. Riff
goes at once to A-rab, like a protective father. The fight is
stopped by a police whistle, louder and louder, and the
arrival of a big goonlike cop, Krupke, and a plainclothes-
man, Schrank. Schrank is strong, always in command; he
has a charming, pleasant manner, which he often employs
to cover his venom and his fear.*

KRUPKE
Knock it off! Settle down.
SCHRANK
All right: *kill each other!* . . . But not on my beat.
RIFF [*such innocence*]
Why if it isn't Lieutenant Schrank!
SEVERAL JETS [*dancing-class manners*]
Top of the day, Lieutenant Schrank.
BERNARDO [*one with Riff*]
And Officer Krupke!
SEVERAL SHARKS
Top of the day, Officer Krupke.
SCHRANK
Boy, what you Puerto Ricans have done to this neighbor-
hood. Which one of 'em clobbered ya, A-rab?
[*A-rab looks to Riff, who takes over with great
helpful seriousness.*]
RIFF
As a matter of factuality, sir, we suspicion the job was done
by a cop.
SNOWBOY
Two cops.

A - R A B

Oh, at least!

K R U P K E

Impossible!

S C H R A N K

Didn't nobody tell ya there's a difference between bein' a
stool pigeon and cooperatin' with the law?

R I F F

You told us the difference, sir. And we all chipped in for
a prize for the first guy who can figure it out.

A C T I O N [*indicating Schrank*]

Maybe buddy boy should get the prize.

S C H R A N K

Don't buddy boy me, Action! I got a hot surprise for you:
you hoodlums don't own the streets. There's been too much
raiding between you and the PRs. All right, Bernardo, get
your trash outa here. [*Mock charm.*] Please.

B E R N A R D O

Let's go, Sharks.   [*They exit.*]

S C H R A N K [*to the Jets*]

If I don't put down the roughhouse, I get put down—on a
traffic corner. Your friend don't like traffic corners. So you
buddy boys are gonna play ball with me. I gotta put up with
them and so do you. *You're gonna make nice with them
PRs from now on.* Because otherwise I'm gonna beat the
crap outa everyone of ya and *then* run ya in. Say good-bye
to the nice boys, Krupke.

K R U P K E

Good-bye, boys.   [*He follows Schrank out.*]

S N O W B O Y [*imitating Krupke*]

Good-bye, boys.

A - R A B

They make a very nice couple.

A C T I O N [*bitterly*]

"You hoodlums don't own the streets."

S N O W B O Y

Go play in the park!

A C T I O N

Keep off the grass!

BABY JOHN
Get outa the house!

ACTION
Keep off the block!

A-RAB
Get outa *here!*

ACTION
Keep off the world! A gang that don't own a street is nuthin'!

RIFF
WE DO OWN IT! Jets—square off! Acemen: [*Diesel, Action and Snowboy line up at attention*] Rocketmen: [*three others line up*] Rank-and-file:

> [*Sheepishly, A-rab trudges into position, Baby John behind him.*]

BABY JOHN [*shocked, to A-rab*]
Gee, your ear's got blood on it!

A-RAB [*proudly*]
I'm a casual, Baby John.

BABY JOHN [*examining the ear*]
Them PRs! They branded you!

SNOWBOY
That makes you a Puerto Rican tomato. Cha-cha-cha, señorita?

RIFF
Cut the frabbajabba. Which one of the Sharks did it?

A-RAB
Bernardo. 'Cause I heard him say: "Thees ees for stink-bombin' my old man's store." [*He makes the same gesture Bernardo made when he pierced his ear.*]

BABY JOHN
Ouch!

ACTION
You shoulda done worse. Them PRs're the reason my old man's gone bust.

RIFF
Who says?

ACTION
My old man says.

BABY JOHN [*to A-rab*]

My old man says his old man woulda gone bust anyway.

ACTION

Your old man says what?

BABY JOHN

My old man says them Puerto Ricans is ruinin' free ennaprise.

ACTION

And what're we doin' about it?

[*Pushing through the gang comes a scrawny teen-age girl, dressed in an outfit that is a pathetic attempt to imitate that of the Jets. Perhaps we have glimpsed her in the fracas before the police came in. Her name is Anybodys.*]

ANYBODYS

Gassin', crabbin'——

ACTION

You still around?

ANYBODYS

Listen, I was a smash in that fight. Oh, Riff, Riff, I was murder!

RIFF

Come on, Anybodys——

ANYBODYS

Riff, how about me gettin' in the gang now?

A-RAB

How about the gang gettin' in——ahhh, who'd wanta!

ANYBODYS

You cheap beast! [*She lunges for A-rab, but Riff pulls her off and pushes her out.*]

RIFF

The road, little lady, the road. [*In a moment of bravado, just before she goes, Anybodys spits—but cautiously.*] Round out! [*This is Riff's summoning of the gang, and they surround him.*] We fought hard for this territory and it's ours. But with those cops servin' as cover, the PRs can move in right under our noses and take it away. *Unless* we speed fast and clean 'em up in one all-out fight!

ACTION [*eagerly*]

A rumble! [*A jabbing gesture.*] Chung! Chung!

RIFF

Cool, Action boy. The Sharks want a place, too, and *they are tough*. They might ask for bottles or knives or zip guns.

BABY JOHN

Zip guns . . . Gee!

RIFF

I'm not finalizin' and sayin' they will: I'm only sayin' they might and we gotta be prepared. Now, what's your mood?

ACTION

I say go, go! !

SNOWBOY

But if they say knives or guns—

BABY JOHN

I say let's forget the whole thing.

DIESEL

What do you say, Riff?

RIFF

I say this turf is small, *but it's all we got*. I wanna hold it like we always held it: with skin! But if they say switch-blades, I'll get a switchblade. I say I want the Jets to be Number One, to sail, to hold the sky!

DIESEL

Then rev us off. [*A punching gesture.*] Voom-va voom!

ACTION

Chung chung!

A-RAB

Cracko, jacko!

SNOWBOY

Riga diga dum!

BABY JOHN

Pam pam! !

RIFF

OK, buddy boys, we rumble! [*General glee.*] Now proto-cality calls for a war council to decide on weapons. I'll make the challenge to Bernardo.

SNOWBOY

You gotta take a lieutenant.

ACTION

That's me!

RIFF

That's Tony.

ACTION

Who needs Tony?

Music starts.

RIFF

Against the Sharks we need every man we got.

ACTION

Tony don't belong any more.

RIFF

Cut it, Action boy. I and Tony started the Jets.

ACTION

Well, he acts like he don't wanna belong.

BABY JOHN

Who wouldn't wanna belong to the Jets!

ACTION

Tony ain't been with us for over a month.

SNOWBOY

What about the day we clobbered the Emeralds?

A-RAB

Which we couldn't have done without Tony.

BABY JOHN

He saved my ever lovin' neck.

RIFF

Right. He's always come through for us and he will now.

[*He sings:*]

When you're a Jet,
You're a Jet all the way
From your first cigarette
To your last dyin' day.
When you're a Jet,
If the spit hits the fan,
You got brothers around,
You're a family man!
You're never alone,
You're never disconnected!
You're home with your own—
When company's expected,
You're well protected!
Then you are set

With a capital J,
Which you'll never forget
Till they cart you away.
When you're a Jet,
You stay
A jet!

[*He speaks:*]

I know Tony like I know me. I guarantee you can count him in.

ACTION

In, out, let's get crackin'.

A-RAB

Where you gonna find Bernardo?

RIFF

At the dance tonight at the gym.

BIG DEAL

But the gym's neutral territory.

RIFF [*sweet innocence*]

I'm gonna make nice there! I'm only gonna challenge him.

RIFF

Great, Daddy-O!

A-RAB

So everybody dress up sweet and sharp. Meet Tony and me at ten. And walk tall!

[*He runs off.*]

A-RAB

We always walk tall!

BABY JOHN

We're Jets!

ACTION

The greatest!

[*He sings with Baby John:*]

When you're a Jet,
You're the top cat in town,
You're the gold-medal kid
With the heavyweight crown!

[*A-rab, Action, Big Deal sing:*]

When you're a Jet,
You're the swingin'est thing.
Little boy, you're a man;

Little boy, you're a king!

[All:]

The Jets are in gear,
Our cylinders are clickin'!
The Sharks'll steer clear
'Cause every Puerto Rican
'S a lousy chicken!

Here come the Jets
Like a bat out of hell—
Someone gets in our way,
Someone don't feel so well!
Here come the Jets:
Little world, step aside!
Better go underground,
Better run, better hide!
We're drawin' the line,
So keep your noses hidden!
We're hangin' a sign
Says "Visitors forbidden"—
And we ain't kiddin'!
Here come the Jets,
Yeah! And we're gonna beat
Every last buggin' gang
On the whole buggin' street!

[Diesel and Action:]

On the whole!

[All:]

Ever—!
Mother—!
Lovin'—!
Street!

The Lights Black Out

SCENE TWO.

5:30 P.M. A back yard.
   *On a small ladder, a good-looking sandy-haired boy is
painting a vertical sign that will say: "Doc's." Below, Riff
is haranguing.*

RIFF

Riga tiga tum tum. Why not? . . . You can't say ya won't,
Tony boy, without sayin' why not?

TONY [grins]

Why not?

RIFF

Because it's me askin': Riff. Womb to tomb!

TONY

Sperm to worm! [Surveying the sign.] You sure this looks
like skywritin'?

RIFF

It's brilliant.

TONY

Twenty-seven years the boss has had that drugstore. I
wanna surprise him with a new sign.

RIFF [shaking the ladder]

Tony, this is important!

TONY

Very important: Acemen, Rocketmen.

RIFF

What's with you? Four and one-half years I live with a
buddy and his family. Four and one-half years I think I
know a man's character. Buddy boy, I am a victim of dis-
appointment in you.

TONY

End your sufferin', little man. Why don't you pack up your
gear and clear out?

RIFF

'Cause your ma's hot for me. [Tony grabs his arm and twists
it.] No! 'Cause I hate livin' with my buggin' uncle uncle
UNCLE!

[Tony releases him and climbs back up the ladder.]

TONY

Now go play nice with the Jets.

RIFF

The Jets are the greatest!

TONY

Were.

RIFF

Are. You found somethin' better?

TONY

No. But—

RIFF

But what?

TONY

You won't dig it.

RIFF

Try me.

TONY

OK ... Every single damn night for the last month, I wake up—and I'm reachin' out.

RIFF

For what?

TONY

I don't know. It's right outside the door, around the corner. But it's comin'!

RIFF

What is? Tell me!

TONY

I don't know! It's—like the kick I used to get from bein' a Jet.

RIFF [*quietly*]

... Or from bein' buddies.

TONY

We're still buddies.

RIFF

The kick comes from people, buddy boy.

TONY

Yeah, but not from being a Jet.

RIFF

No? Without a gang you're an orphan. With a gang you walk in two's, three's, four's. And when your gang is the best, when you're a Jet, buddy boy, you're out in the sun and home free home!

TONY

Riff, I've had it. [*Pause.*]

RIFF

Tony, the trouble is large: the Sharks bite hard! We got to stop them now, and we need *you!* [*Pause. Quietly.*] I never

asked the time of day from a clock, but I'm askin' you:
Come to the dance tonight . . . [*Tony turns away.*] . . . I
already told the gang you'd be there.

TONY [*after a moment, turns to him with a grin*]
What time?

RIFF
Ten?

TONY
Ten it is.

RIFF
Womb to tomb!

TONY
Sperm to worm! And I'll live to regret this.

RIFF
Who knows? Maybe what you're waitin' for'll be twitchin'
at the dance!

[*He runs off.*]

TONY
Who knows?

[*Music starts and he sings:*]

Could be! . . .
Who knows? . . .
There's something due any day;
I will know right away
Soon as it shows.
It may come cannonballin' down through the sky,
Gleam in its eye,
Bright as a rose!
Who knows? . . .
It's only just out of reach,
Down the block, on a beach,
Under a tree.
I got a feeling there's a miracle due,
Gonna come true,
Coming to me!

Could it be? Yes, it could.
Something's coming, something good,
If I can wait!
Something's coming, I don't know what it is

But it is
Gonna be great!

With a click, with a shock,
Phone'll jingle, door'll knock,
Open the latch!
Something's coming, don't know when, but it's soon—
Catch the moon,
One-handed catch!

Around the corner,
Or whistling down the river,
Come on—deliver
To me!

Will it be? Yes, it will.
Maybe just by holding still
It'll be there!
Come on, something, come on in, don't be shy,
Meet a guy,
Pull up a chair!

The air is humming,
And something great is coming!
Who knows?
It's only just out of reach,
Down the block, on a beach . . .
Maybe tonight . . .

The Lights Dim

SCENE THREE.

6:00 P.M. A bridal shop.
  A small section, enough to include a table with sewing machine, a chair or two.

*Anita, a Puerto Rican girl with loose hair and slightly
flashy clothes, is finishing remaking what was a white com-
munion dress into a party dress for an extremely lovely,
extremely young girl: Maria. Anita is knowing, sexual,
sharp. Maria is an excited, enthusiastic, obedient child, with
the temper, stubborn strength and awareness of a woman.*

MARIA [*holding out scissors*]
Por favor, Anita. Make the neck lower!
ANITA
Stop it, Maria.
MARIA
One inch. How much can one little inch do?
ANITA
Too much.
MARIA [*exasperated*]
Anita, it is now to be a dress for dancing, no longer for
kneeling in front of an altar.
ANITA
With those boys you can start in dancing and end up
kneeling.
MARIA
Querida, one little inch; *una poca poca*—
ANITA
Bernardo made me promise—
MARIA
Ai! Bernardo! One month have I been in this country—do
I ever even touch excitement? I sew all day, I sit all night.
For what did my fine brother bring me here?
ANITA
To marry Chino.
MARIA
When I look at Chino, nothing happens.
ANITA
What do you expect to happen?
MARIA
I don't know: something. What happens when you look at
Bernardo?
ANITA
It's when I don't look that it happens.

MARIA

I think I will tell Mama and Papa about you and 'Nardo in the balcony of the movies.

ANITA

I'll rip this to shreds!

MARIA

No. But if you perhaps could manage to lower the neck—

ANITA

Next year.

MARIA

Next year I will be married and no one will care if it is down to here!

ANITA

Down to where?

MARIA

Down to here. [*Indicates her waist.*] I hate this dress!

ANITA

Then don't wear it and don't come with us to the dance.

MARIA [*shocked*]

Don't come! [*Grabs the dress.*] Could we not dye it red, at least?

ANITA

No, we could not. [*She starts to help Maria into the dress.*]

MARIA

White is for babies. I will be the only one there in a white—

ANITA

Well ? ? ?

MARIA

Ahhhh—*sí!* It is a beautiful dress: I love you!

[*As she hugs Anita, Bernardo enters, followed by a shy, gentle sweet-faced boy: Chino.*]

BERNARDO

Are you ready?

MARIA

Come in, 'Nardo. [*Whirls in the dress.*] Is it not beautiful?

BERNARDO [*looking only at Maria's face*]

Yes. [*Kisses her.*] Very.

ANITA

I didn't quite hear . . .

BERNARDO [*kissing Anita quite differently*]
Very beautiful.

MARIA
[*watches them a second, then turns to Chino*]
Come in, Chino. Do not be afraid.

CHINO
But this is a shop for ladies.

BERNARDO
Our ladies!

MARIA
'Nardo, it is most important that I have a wonderful time at the dancing tonight.

BERNARDO [*as Anita hooks up Maria*]
Why?

MARIA
Because tonight is the real beginning of my life as a young lady of America!
[*She begins to whirl in the dress as the shop slides off and a flood of gaily colored streamers pours down. As Maria begins to turn and turn, going off-stage, Shark girls, dressed for the dance whirl on, followed by Jet girls, by boys from both gangs. The streamers fly up again for the next scene.*]

SCENE FOUR.

10:00 P.M. The gym.

Actually, a converted gymnasium of a settlement house, at the moment being used as a dancehall, disguised for the occasion with streamers and bunting.

Both gangs are jitterbugging wildly with their bodies, but their faces, although they are enjoying themselves, remain cool, almost detached. The line between the two gangs is sharply defined by the colors they wear: the Jets, girls as

*well as boys, reflecting the colors of the Jet jackets; the same
is true of the Sharks. The dancing is a physical and emotional release for these kids.*

*Maria enters with Chino, Bernardo and Anita. As she
looks around, delighted, thrilled by this, her first dance, the
Jets catch sight of Bernardo, who is being greeted by Pepe,
his lieutenant, and other Sharks. As the music peters away,
the Jets withdraw to one side of the hall, around Riff. The
Sharks, seeing this, draw to their side, around Bernardo. A
brief consultation, and Riff starts across—with lieutenants
—to make his challenge to Bernardo, who starts—with his
lieutenants—to meet him. The moment is brief but it would
be disastrous if a smiling, overly cheerful young man of
about thirty did not hurry forward. He is called Glad Hand,
and he is a "square."*

GLAD HAND [*beaming*]
All right, boys and girls! Attention, please! [*Hum of talk.*]
Attention! [*Krupke appears behind Glad Hand: the talk
stops.*] Thank you. It sure is a fine turnout tonight. [*Ad libs
from the kids.*] We want you to make friends here, so we're
going to have a few get-together dances. [*Ad libs: "Oh,
ginger peachy," etc.*] You form two circles: boys on the
outside, girls on the inside.
SNOWBOY
Where are you?
GLAD HAND [*tries to laugh at this*]
All right. Now when the music stops, each boy dances with
whichever girl is opposite. O.K.? O.K. Two circles, kids.
[*The kids clap their hands back at him and ad lib: "Two
circles, kids," etc., but do not move.*] Well, it won't hurt you
to try.
SNOWBOY [*limping forward*]
Oh, it hurts; it hurts; it—
  [*Krupke steps forward. Snowboy straightens up and
  meekly returns to his place. Riff steps forward and
  beckons to his girl, Velma. She is terribly young,
  sexy, lost in a world of jive. She slithers forward to
  take her place with Riff. The challenge is met by*

> *Bernardo, who steps forward, leading Anita as*
> *though he were presenting the most magnificent lady*
> *in all the world. The other kids follow, forming the*
> *two circles Glad Hand requested.*]

GLAD HAND

That's it, kids. Keep the ball rolling. Round she goes and
where she stops, nobody knows. All right: here we go!

> [*Promenade music starts and the circles start re-*
> *volving. Glad Hand, whistle to his mouth, is in the*
> *center with Krupke. He blows the whistle and the*
> *music stops, leaving Jet boys opposite Shark girls,*
> *and vice versa. There is a moment of tenseness, then*
> *Bernardo reaches across the Jet girl opposite for*
> *Anita's hand, and she comes to him. Riff reaches for*
> *Velma; and the kids of both gangs follow suit. The*
> *"get-together" has failed, and each gang is on its*
> *own side of the hall as a mambo starts. This turns*
> *into a challenge dance between Bernardo and Anita*
> *—cheered on by the Sharks—and Riff and Velma—*
> *cheered on by the Jets. During it, Tony enters and*
> *is momentarily embraced by Riff, who is delighted*
> *that his best friend did turn up. The dance builds*
> *wilder and wilder, until, at the peak, everybody is*
> *dancing and shouting, "Go, Mambo!" It is at this*
> *moment that Tony and Maria—at opposite sides of*
> *the hall—see each other. They have been cheering*
> *on their respective friends, clapping in rhythm. Now,*
> *as they see each other, their voices die, their smiles*
> *fade, their hands slowly go to their sides. The lights*
> *fade on the others, who disappear into the haze of*
> *the background as a delicate cha-cha begins and*
> *Tony and Maria slowly walk forward to meet each*
> *other. Slowly, as though in a dream, they drift into*
> *the steps of the dance, always looking at each other,*
> *completely lost in each other; unaware of anyone,*
> *any place, any time, anything but one another.*]

TONY

You're not thinking I'm someone else?

MARIA

I know you are not.

TONY

Or that we have met before?

MARIA

I know we have not.

TONY

I felt, I *knew* something-never-before was going to happen, had to happen. But this is—

MARIA [*interrupting*]

My hands are cold. [*He takes them in his.*] Yours, too. [*He moves her hands to his face.*] So warm. [*She moves his hands to her face.*]

TONY

Yours, too.

MARIA

But of course. They are the same.

TONY

It's so much to believe—you're not joking me?

MARIA

I have not yet learned how to joke that way. I think now I never will.

> [*Impulsively, he stops to kiss her hands; then tenderly, innocently, her lips. The music bursts out, the lights flare up, and Bernardo is upon them in an icy rage.*]

BERNARDO

Go home, "American."

TONY

Slow down, Bernardo.

BERNARDO

Stay away from my sister!

TONY

...Sister?

[*Riff steps up.*]

BERNARDO [*to Maria*]

Couldn't you see he's one of them?

MARIA

No; I saw only him.

BERNARDO [*as Chino comes up*]

I told you: there's only one thing they want from a Puerto Rican girl!

TONY

That's a lie!

RIFF

Cool, boy.

CHINO [to Tony]

Get away.

TONY

You keep out, Chino. [To Maria:] Don't listen to them!

BERNARDO

She will listen to her brother before—

RIFF [overlapping]

If you characters want to settle—

GLAD HAND

Please! Everything was going so well! Do you fellows get pleasure out of making trouble? Now come on—it won't hurt you to have a good time.

> [Music starts again. Bernardo is on one side with Maria and Chino; Anita joins them. Tony is on the other with Riff and Diesel. Light emphasizes the first group.]

BERNARDO

I warned you—

CHINO

Do not yell at her, 'Nardo.

BERNARDO

You yell at babies.

ANITA

And put ideas in the baby's head.

BERNARDO

Take her home, Chino.

MARIA

'Nardo, it is my first dance.

BERNARDO

Please. We are family, Maria. Go.

> [Maria hesitates, then starts out with Chino as the light follows her to the other group, which she passes.]

RIFF [to Diesel, indicating Tony happily]

I guess the kid's with us for sure now.

[*Tony doesn t even hear; he is staring at Maria, who stops for a moment.*]

CHINO

Come, Maria.

[*They continue out.*]

TONY

Maria . . .

[*He is unaware that Bernardo is crossing toward him, but Riff intercepts.*]

BERNARDO

I don't want you.

RIFF

I want you, though. For a war council—Jets and Sharks.

BERNARDO

The pleasure is mine.

RIFF

Let's go outside.

BERNARDO

I would not leave the ladies here alone. We will meet you in half an hour.

RIFF

Doc's drugstore? [*Bernardo nods.*] And no jazz before then.

BERNARDO

I understand the rules—Native Boy.

[*The light is fading on them, on everyone but Tony.*]

RIFF

Spread the word, Diesel.

DIESEL

Right, Daddy-o.

RIFF

Let's get the chicks and kick it. Tony?

TONY

Maria . . .

[*Music starts.*]

RIFF [*in darkness*]

Tony!

DIESEL [*in darkness*]

Ah, we'll see him at Doc's.

TONY [*speaking dreamily over the music—he is now standing alone in the light*]

Maria . . .

[*Singing softly:*]

The most beautiful sound I ever heard.
>   VOICES [*offstage:*]
Maria, Maria, Maria, Maria . . .
>   TONY
All the beautiful sounds of the world in a single word:
>   VOICES [*offstage:*]
Maria, Maria, Maria, Maria . . .

[*Swelling in intensity.*]

Maria, Maria . . .
>   TONY
Maria!
I've just met a girl named Maria,
And suddenly that name
Will never be the same
To me.

Maria!
I've just kissed a girl named Maria,
And suddenly I've found
How wonderful a sound
Can be!

Maria!
Say it loud and there's music playing—
Say it soft and it's almost like praying—
Maria . . .
I'll never stop saying
Maria!
>   CHORUS [*offstage, against Tony's obbligato:*]
I've just met a girl named Maria,
And suddenly that name
Will never be the same
To me.
Maria—
I've just kissed a girl named Maria,
And suddenly I've found
How wonderful a sound
Can be!

TONY

Maria—
Say it loud and there's music playing—
Say it soft and it's almost like praying—
Maria—
I'll never stop saying Maria!
The most beautiful sound I ever heard—
Maria.

> [During the song, the stage behind Tony has gone
> dark; by the time he has finished, it is set for the
> next scene.]

SCENE FIVE.

11:00 P.M. A back alley.

*A suggestion of buildings; a fire escape climbing to the
rear window of an unseen flat.*

*As Tony sings, he looks for where Maria lives, wishing
for her. And she does appear, at the window above him,
which opens onto the fire escape. Music stays beneath most
of the scene.*

TONY [sings:]

Maria, Maria . . .

MARIA

Ssh!

TONY

Maria! !

MARIA

Quiet!

TONY

Come down.

MARIA

No.

TONY

Maria . . .

MARIA

Please. If Bernardo—

TONY

He's at the dance. Come down.

MARIA

He will soon bring Anita home.

TONY

Just for a minute.

MARIA [smiles]

A minute is not enough.

TONY [smiles]

For an hour, then.

MARIA

I cannot.

TONY

Forever!

MARIA

Ssh!

TONY

Then I'm coming up.

WOMAN'S VOICE [from the offstage apartment]

Maria!

MARIA

Momentito, Mama . . .

TONY [climbing up]

Maria, Maria—

MARIA

Cállate! [Reaching her hand out to stop him.] Ssh!

TONY [grabbing her hand]

Ssh!

MARIA

It is dangerous.

TONY

I'm not "one of them."

MARIA

You are; but to me, you are not. Just as I am one of them—
[She gestures toward the apartment.]

TONY

To me, you are all the—
> [*She covers his mouth with her hand.*]

MAN'S VOICE [*from the unseen apartment*]

Maruca!

MARIA

Sí, ya vengo, Papa.

TONY

Maruca?

MARIA

His pet name for me.

TONY

I like him. He will like me.

MARIA

No. He is like Bernardo: afraid. [*Suddenly laughing.*]
Imagine being afraid of you!

TONY

You see?

MARIA [*touching his face*]

I see you.

TONY

See only me.

MARIA [*sings:*]

Only you, you're the only thing I'll see forever.
In my eyes, in my words and in everything I do,
Nothing else but you
Ever!

TONY

And there's nothing for me but Maria,
Every sight that I see is Maria.

MARIA

Tony, Tony . . .

TONY

Always you, every thought I'll ever know,
Everywhere I go, you'll be.

MARIA

All the world is only you and me!
> [*And now the buildings, the world fade away,
> leaving them suspended in space.*]

Tonight, tonight,
It all began tonight,
I saw you and the world went away.
Tonight, tonight,
There's only you tonight,
What you are, what you do, what you say.

TONY

Today, all day I had the feeling
A miracle would happen—
I know now I was right.
For here you are
And what was just a world is a star
Tonight!

BOTH

Tonight, tonight,
The world is full of light,
With suns and moons all over the place.
Tonight, tonight,
The world is wild and bright,
Going mad, shooting sparks into space.
Today the world was just an address,
A place for me to live in,
No better than all right,
But here you are
And what was just a world is a star
Tonight!

MAN'S VOICE [offstage]

Maruca!

MARIA

Wait for me! [She goes inside as the buildings begin to come back into place.]

TONY [sings]

Tonight, tonight,
It all began tonight,
I saw you and the world went away.

MARIA [returning]

I cannot stay. Go quickly!

TONY

I'm not afraid.

MARIA

They are strict with me. Please.

TONY [*kissing her*]

Good night.

MARIA

Buenas noches.

TONY

I love you.

MARIA

Yes, yes. Hurry. [*He climbs down.*] Wait! When will I see
you? [*He starts back up.*] No!

TONY

Tomorrow.

MARIA

I work at the bridal shop. Come there.

TONY

At sundown.

MARIA

Yes. Good night.

TONY

Good night. [*He starts off.*]

MARIA

Tony!

TONY

Ssh!

MARIA

Come to the back door.

TONY

Sí. [*Again he starts out.*]

MARIA

Tony! [*He stops. A pause.*] What does Tony stand for?

TONY

Anton.

MARIA

Te adoro, Anton.

TONY

Te adoro, Maria.

[*Both sing as music starts again:*]

Good night, good night,
Sleep well and when you dream,

Dream of me
Tonight.

> [*She goes inside; He ducks out into the shadows just as Bernardo and Anita enter, followed by Indio, and Pepe and their girls. One is a bleached-blond, bangled beauty: Consuelo. The other, more quietly dressed, is Rosalia. She is not too bright.*]

BERNARDO [*Looking up to the window*]

Maria?

ANITA

She *has* a mother. Also a father.

BERNARDO

They do not know this country any better than she does.

ANITA

You do not know it at all! Girls here are free to have fun. She-is-in-America-now.

BERNARDO [*exaggerated*]

But Puerto-Rico-is-in-America-now!

ANITA [*in disgust*]

Ai!

BERNARDO [*cooing*]

Anita Josefina Teresita—

ANITA

It's plain Anita now—

BERNARDO [*continuing through*]

—Beatriz del Carmen Margarita, etcetera, etcetera—

ANITA

Immigrant!

BERNARDO [*pulling her to him*]

Thank God, you can't change your hair!

PEPE [*fondling Consuelo's bleached mop*]

Is that possible?

CONSUELO

In the U.S.A., everything is real.

BERNARDO [*to Chino, who enters*]

Chino, how was she when you took her home?

CHINO

All right. 'Nardo, she was only dancing.

BERNARDO

With an "*American*." Who is really a Polack.

ANITA

Says the Spic.

BERNARDO

You are not so cute.

ANITA

That Tony is.

ROSALIA

And he works.

CHINO

A delivery boy.

ANITA

And what are you?

CHINO

An assistant.

BERNARDO

Si! And Chino makes half what the Polack makes—the Polack is American!

ANITA

Ai! Here comes the whole commercial! [*A burlesque oration in mock Puerto Rican accent. Bernardo starts the first line with her.*] The mother of Tony was born in Poland; the father still goes to night school. Tony was born in America, so that makes him an American. But us? Foreigners!

PEPE *and* CONSUELO

Lice!

PEPE, CONSUELO, ANITA

Cockroaches!

BERNARDO

Well, it is true! You remember how we were when we first came! Did we even think of going back?

BERNARDO *and* ANITA

No! We came ready, eager—

ANITA [*mocking*]

With our hearts open—

CONSUELO

Our arms open—

PEPE

You came with your pants open.

CONSUELO

You did, pig! [*Slaps him.*] You'll go back with handcuffs!

BERNARDO
I am going back with a Cadillac!
CHINO
Air-conditioned!
BERNARDO
Built-in bar!
CHINO
Telephone!
BERNARDO
Television!
CHINO
Compatible color!
BERNARDO
And a king-sized bed. [*Grabs Anita.*] Come on.
ANITA [*mimicking*]
Come on.
BERNARDO
Well, are you or aren't you?
ANITA
Well, are you or aren't you?
BERNARDO
Well, are you?
ANITA
You have your big, important war council. The council or
me?
BERNARDO
First one, then the other.
ANITA [*breaking away from him*]
I am an American girl now. I don't wait.
BERNARDO [*to Chino*]
Back home, women know their place.
ANITA
Back home, little boys don't have war councils.
BERNARDO
You want me to be an American? [*To the boys.*] *Vámonos,
chicos, Es tarde.* [*A mock bow.*] *Buenos noches,* Anita
Josefina del Carmen, etcetera, etcetera, etcetera.
                              [*He exits with the boys.*]
ROSALIA
That's a very pretty name: Etcetera.

ANITA

Ai!

CONSUELO

She means well.

ROSALIA

We have many pretty names at home.

ANITA [*mimicking*]

At home, at home. If it's so nice "at home," why don't you go back there?

ROSALIA

I would like to—[*A look from Anita.*]—just for a successful visit.

[*She sings nostalgically:*]

Puerto Rico . . .
You lovely island . . .
Island of tropical breezes.
    Always the pineapples growing,
    Always the coffee blossoms blowing . . .

ANITA [*sings sarcastically*]

Puerto Rico . . .
You ugly island . . .
Island of tropic diseases.
    Always the hurricanes blowing,
    Always the population growing . . .
    And the money owing,
    And the babies crying,
    And the bullets flying.
I like the island Manhattan—
Smoke on your pipe and put that in!

[*all, except Rosalia:*]

I like to be in America!
OK by me in America!
Everything free in America
For a small fee in America!

ROSALIA

I like the city of San Juan—

ANITA

I know a boat you can get on.

ROSALIA

Hundreds of flowers in full bloom—

ANITA

Hundreds of people in each room!

[*All, except Rosalia:*]

Automobile in America,
Chromium steel in America,
Wire-spoke wheel in America—
Very big deal in America!

ROSALIA

I'll drive a Buick through San Juan—

ANITA

If there's a road you can drive on.

ROSALIA

I'll give my cousins a free ride—

ANITA

How you get all of them inside?

[*All, except Rosalia:*]

Immigrant goes to America,
Many hellos in America;
Nobody knows in America
Puerto Rico's in America.

[*The girls whistle and dance.*]

ROSALIA

When will I go back to San Juan—

ANITA

When you will shut up and get gone!

ROSALIA

I'll give them new washing machine—

ANITA

What have they got there to keep clean?

[*All, except Rosalia:*]

I like the shores of America!
Comfort is yours in America!
Knobs on the doors in America,
Wall-to-wall floors in America!

[*They whistle and dance.*]

ROSALIA

I'll bring a TV to San Juan—

ANITA

If there's a current to turn on.

ROSALIA

Everyone there will give big cheer!

ANITA

Everyone there will have moved here!

> [*The song ends in a joyous dance.*]
> The Lights Black Out

SCENE SIX.

Midnight. The drugstore.

A suggestion of a run-down, musty general store which, in cities, is called a drugstore. A door leading to the street outside; another leading to the cellar below.

Baby John is reading a comic book; A-rab is playing solitaire; Anybodys is huddled by the jukebox; Action is watching the street door. The atmosphere is tense, jumpy. Action slams the door and strides to the dart board.

ACTION

Where the devil are they? Are we havin' a war council tonight or ain't we? [*He throws a dart savagely.*]

BABY JOHN

He don't use knives. He don't even use an atomic ray gun.

A-RAB

Who don't?

BABY JOHN

Superman. Gee, I love him.

SNOWBOY

So marry him.

ANYBODYS

I ain't never gonna get married: too noisy.

A-RAB

You ain't never gonna get married: too ugly.

ANYBODYS [*"shooting" him*]

Pow pow!

A-RAB

Cracko, jacko! [*Clutching his belly, he spins to the floor.*]
Down goes a teen-age hoodlum.

BABY JOHN

Could a zip gun make you do like that?
[*A second of silence. Then Snowboy slams into the room
and they all jump.*]

ACTION

What the hell's a matter with you?

SNOWBOY

I got caught sneakin' outa the movies.

A-RAB

Sneaking' *out?* Whadd'ya do that for?

SNOWBOY

I sneaked in.

ACTION

A war council comin' up and he goes to the movies.

ANYBODYS

And you let him be a Jet!

BABY JOHN

Ah, go walk the streets like ya sister.

ANYBODYS [*jumping him*]

Lissen, jail bait, I licked you twice and I can do it again.
[*From the doorway behind the counter a little middle-aged
man enters: Doc.*]

DOC

Curfew, gentlemen. And lady. Baby John, you should be
home in bed.

BABY JOHN

We're gonna have a war council here, Doc.

DOC

A who?

A-RAB

To decide on weapons for a big-time rumble!

SNOWBOY

We're gonna mix with the PRs.

DOC

Weapons. You couldn't play basketball?

ANYBODYS

Get with it, buddy boy.

DOC

War councils—

ACTION

Don't start, Doc.

DOC

Rumbles . . .

ACTION

Doc—

DOC

Why, when I was your age—

ACTION

When you was my age; when my old man was my age; when my brother was my age! *You was never my age, none a you!* The sooner you creeps get hip to that, the sooner you'll dig us.

DOC

I'll dig your early graves, that's what I'll dig.

A-RAB

Dig, dig, dig—

DOC

What're you gonna be when you grow up?

ANYBODYS [*wistfully.*]

A telephone call girl!

[*The store doorbell tinkles as Riff enters with Velma.*]

SNOWBOY

Riff, hey!

ACTION

Are they comin'?

RIFF

Unwind, Action. Hey, Doc, Tony here?

DOC

No, Riff, it's closing time.

ACTION [*to Riff*]

What d'ya think they're gonna ask for?

A-RAB

Just rubber hoses, maybe, huh?

RIFF

Cool, little men. Easy, freezy cool.

VELMA

Oo, oo, ooblee—oo.

[*Diesel enters with a would-be grand number: Graziella.*]

DIESEL

They're comin' any minute now!

ACTION

Chung chung!

A-RAB

Cracko, jacko!

VELMA

Ooblee-oo.

RIFF [*sharply*]

Cool!

ANYBODYS

Riff—in a tight spot you need every man you can—

RIFF

No.

GRAZIELLA [*indicating Anybodys to Velma*]

An American tragedy.

ANYBODYS ["*shooting*" *her*]

Pow.

GRAZIELLA

Poo.

VELMA

Ooblee-pooh.

[*They giggle.*]

RIFF

Now when the victims come in, you chicks cut out.

GRAZIELLA

We might, and then again we might not.

DIESEL

This ain't kid stuff, Graziella.

GRAZIELLA

I and Velma ain't kid stuff, neither. Are we, Vel?

VELMA

No thank you-oo, ooblee-oo.

GRAZIELLA

And you can punctuate it?

VELMA

Ooo!

[*They giggle again.*]

ACTION [to Riff]

What're we poopin' around with dumb broads?

GRAZIELLA [enraged]

I and Velma ain't dumb!

ACTION

We got important business comin'.

DOC

Makin' trouble for the Puerto Ricans?

SNOWBOY

They make trouble for us.

DOC

Look! He almost laughs when he says it. For you, trouble is a relief.

RIFF

We've got to stand up to the PRs, Doc. It's important.

DOC

Fighting over a little piece of the street is so important?

ACTION

To us, it is.

DOC

To hoodlums, it is. [He goes out through the cellar doorway as Action lunges for him.]

ACTION

Don't you call me hoodlum!

RIFF [holding him]

Easy, Action! Save your steam for the rumble.

A-RAB

He don't want what we want, so we're hoodlums!

BABY JOHN

I wear a jacket like my buddies, so my teacher calls me hoodlum!

ACTION

I swear the next creep who calls me hoodlum—

RIFF

You'll laugh! Yeah. Now you all better dig this and dig it the most. No matter who or what is eatin' at you, you show it, buddy boys, and you are dead. You are cuttin' a hole in yourselves for them to stick in a red-hot umbrella and open it. Wide. You wanna live? You play it cool.

[Music starts.]

ACTION

I wanna get even!

RIFF

Get cool.

A-RAB

I wanna bust!

RIFF

Bust cool.

BABY JOHN

I wanna go!

RIFF

Go cool!

Boy, boy, crazy boy—   [*He sings:*]
    Get cool, boy!
Got a rocket in your pocket—
    Keep coolly cool, boy!
        Don't get hot,
        'Cause, man, you got
        Some high times ahead.
    Take it slow and, Daddy-o,
        You can live it up and die in bed!
Boy, boy, crazy boy—
    Stay loose, boy!
Breeze it, buzz it, easy does it—
    Turn off the juice, boy!
        Go man, go,
        But not like a yo
        Yo school boy—
        Just play it cool, boy,
Real cool!
Easy, Action.
Easy.

> [*This leads into a frenetic dance in which the boys
> and girls release their emotions and get "cool." It
> finishes, starts again when a Jet bounces in with the
> gang whistle. Everyone but Riff and Velma stops
> dancing. A moment, then Bernardo, Chino, Pepe
> and Indio enter. The tinkle of the doorbell brings a
> worried Doc back in. Tension—but Riff dances a
> moment longer. Then he pats Velma on her behind.*

*Followed by Graziella, she runs out, slithering past
the Sharks. Anybodys is back, huddled by the jukebox, but Riff spots her. She gives him a pleading let-
me-stay look, but he gestures for her to go. Unlike
the other girls, as she exits, Anybodys shoves the
Sharks like a big tough man.]*

RIFF

Set 'em up, Doc. Cokes all around.

BERNARDO

Let's get down to business.

RIFF

Bernardo hasn't learned the procedures of gracious livin'.

BERNARDO

I don't like you, either. So cut it.

RIFF

Kick it, Doc.

DOC

Boys, couldn't you maybe all talk it——

RIFF

Kick it!

*[Doc goes out. The two gangs take places behind
their leaders.]*.

RIFF

We challenge you to a rumble. All out, once and for all.
Accept?

BERNARDO

On what terms?

RIFF

Whatever terms you're callin', buddy boy. You crossed the
line once too often.

BERNARDO

You started it.

RIFF

Who jumped A-rab this afternoon?

BERNARDO

Who jumped me the first day I moved here?

ACTION

Who asked you to move here?

PEPE

Who asked you?

SNOWBOY

Move where you're wanted!

A-RAB

Back where ya came from!

ACTION

Spics!

PEPE

Micks!

INDIO

Wop!

BERNARDO

We accept!

RIFF

Time:

BERNARDO

Tomorrow?

RIFF

After dark. [*They shake.*] Place:

BERNARDO

The park.

RIFF

The river.

BERNARDO

Under the highway.

[*They shake.*]

RIFF

Weapons:

[*The doorbell tinkles as Tony bursts in, yelling.*]

TONY

Hay, Doc!

[*He stops as he sees them. Silence. Then he comes forward.*]

RIFF

Weapons!

[*Doc enters.*]

BERNARDO

Weapons . . .

RIFF

You call.

BERNARDO

Your challenge.

RIFF

Afraid to call?

BERNARDO

... Sticks.

RIFF

... Rocks.

BERNARDO

... Poles.

RIFF

... Cans.

BERNARDO

... Bricks.

RIFF

... Bats.

BERNARDO

... Clubs.

RIFF

Chains.

TONY

Bottles, knives, guns! [*They stare.*] What a coop full of chickens!

ACTION

Who you callin' chicken?

BERNARDO

Every dog knows his own.

TONY

I'm callin' all of you chicken. The big tough buddy boys have to throw bricks! Afraid to get close in? Afraid to slug it out? Afraid to use plain skin?

BABY JOHN

Not even garbage?

ACTION

That ain't a rumble.

RIFF

Who says?

BERNARDO

You said call weapons.

TONY

A rumble can be clinched by a fair fight. If you have the guts to risk that. Best man from each gang to slug it out.

BERNARDO [*looking at Tony*]

I'd enjoy to risk that. O.K.! Fair fight!

PEPE

What?

ACTION [*simultaneously*]

No!

RIFF

The commanders say yes or no. [*To Bernardo.*] Fair fight.
[*They shake.*]

BERNARDO [*to Tony*]

In two minutes you will be like a fish after skinnin'.

RIFF

Your best man fights our best man—and we pick him.
[*Claps Diesel on the shoulder.*]

BERNARDO

But I thought I would be—

RIFF

We shook on it, Bernardo.

BERNARDO

Yes. I shook on it.

ACTION [*quickly*]

Look, Bernardo, if you wanna change your mind, maybe we could all—

[*One of the Jets near the door suddenly whistles. Instantly, they shift positions so they are mixed up: no segregation. Silence; then in comes Schrank. During the following, the gangs are absolutely silent and motionless, unless otherwise indicated.*]

DOC [*unhappily*]

Good evening, Lieutenant Schrank. I and Tony was just closing up.

SCHRANK [*lifting a pack of cigarettes*]

Mind?

DOC

I have no mind. I am the village idiot.

SCHRANK [*lighting a cigarette*]

I always make it a rule to smoke in the can. And what else

is a room with half-breeds in it, eh, Riff? [*Bernado's move is checked by Riff. Schrank speaks again, pleasantly.*] Clear out, Spics. Sure; it's a free country and I ain't got the right. But it's a country with laws: and I can find the right. I got the badge, you got the skin. It's tough all over. Beat it! [*A second. Then Riff nods once to Bernardo, who nods to his gang. Slowly, they file out. Bernardo starts to whistle "My Country 'Tis of Thee" as he exits proudly. His gang joins in, finishing a sardonic jazz lick offstage. Schrank, still pleasant.*] From their angle, sure. Say, where's the rumble gonna be? Ah, look: I know regular Americans don't rub with the gold-teeth otherwise. The river? The park? [*Silence.*] I'm for *you.* I want this beat cleaned up and you can do it for me. I'll even lend a hand if it gets rough. Where ya gonna rumble? The playground? Sweeney's lot? [*Angered by the silence.*] Ya think I'm a lousy stool pigeon? I wanna help ya get rid of them! Come on! Where's it gonna be? . . . Get smart, you stupid hoodlums! I oughta fine ya for litterin' the streets. You oughta be taken down the station house and have your skulls mashed to a pulp! You and the tin-horn immigrant scum you come from! How's your old man's d.t.'s, A-rab? How's the action on your mother's mattress, Action? [*Action lunges for him but is tripped up by Riff. Schrank crouches low, ready for him. Quiet now.*] Let him go, buddy boy, just let him go. [*Action starts to his feet but Diesel holds him.*] One of these days there won't be nobody to hold you. [*Riff deliberately starts for the door, followed by the others, except Tony.*] I'll find out where ya gonna rumble. But be sure to finish each other off. Because if you don't, I will! [*Riff has stayed at the door until the others have passed through. Now he just looks at Schrank and cockily saunters out. Silence. Schrank looks at Doc.*] Well, you try keepin' hoodlums in line and see what it does to you.   [*He exits.*]

> DOC [*indicating Schrank*]

It wouldn't give me a mouth like his.

> TONY

Forget him. From here on in, everything goes my way. [*He starts to clean up, to turn out the lights.*]

DOC

You think it'll really be a fair fight.

TONY

Yeah.

DOC

What have you been takin' tonight?

TONY

A trip to the moon. And I'll tell you a secret. It isn't a man that's up there, Doc. It's a girl, a lady. [*Opens the door.*] *Buenas noches, señor.*

DOC

Buenas noches?! So that's why you made it a fair fight. [*Tony smiles.*] . . . Tony . . . things aren't tough enough?

TONY

Tough? Doc, I'm in love.

DOC

How do you know?

TONY

Because . . . there isn't any other way I could feel.

DOC

And you're not frightened?

TONY

Should I be?

[*He opens door, exits.*]

DOC

Why? I'm frightened enough for both of you. [*He turns out the last light.*]

The Stage is Dark

SCENE SEVEN.

5:30 P.M. The next day. The bridal shop.

   Hot late-afternoon sun coloring the workroom. One or two sewing machines. Several dressmaker dummies, male and female, in bridal-party garb.

Maria, in a smock is hand-sewing a wedding veil as Anita whirls in whipping off her smock.

ANITA

She's gone! The old bag of a *bruja* has gone!

MARIA

Bravo!

ANITA

The day is over, the jail is open, home we go!

MARIA

You go, *querida.* I will lock up.

ANITA

Finish tomorrow. Come!

MARIA

But I am in no hurry.

ANITA

I am. I'm going to take a bubble bath all during supper: Black Orchid.

MARIA

You will not eat?

ANITA

After the rumble—with 'Nardo.

MARIA [*sewing, angrily*]

That rumble, why do they have it?

ANITA

You saw how they dance: like they have to get rid of something, quick. That's how they fight.

MARIA

To get rid of what?

ANITA

Too much feeling. And they get rid of it: after a fight, that brother of yours is so healthy! Definitely: Black Orchid.

[*There is a knock at rear door, and Tony enters.*]

TONY

Buenas noches!

ANITA [*sarcastically, to Maria*]

"You go, *querida.* I will lock up." [*To Tony:*] It's too early for *noches. Buenas tardes.*

TONY [*bows*]

Gracias. Buenas tardes.

MARIA

He just came to deliver aspirin.

ANITA

You'll need it.

TONY

No, we're out of the world.

ANITA

You're out of your heads.

TONY

We're twelve feet in the air.

MARIA [*gently taking his hand*]

Anita can see all that. [*To Anita:*] You will not tell?

ANITA

Tell what? How can I hear what goes on twelve feet over my head? [*Opens door. To Maria:*] You better be home in fifteen minutes.

[*She goes out.*]

TONY

Don't worry. She likes us!

MARIA

But she is worried.

TONY

She's foolish. We're untouchable; we *are* in the air; we have magic!

MARIA

Magic is also evil and black. Are you going to that rumble?

TONY

No.

MARIA

Yes.

TONY

Why? ?

MARIA

You must go and stop it.

TONY

I have stopped it! It's only a fist fight. 'Nardo won't get—

MARIA

Any fight is not good for us.

TONY

Everything is good for us and we are good for everything.

MARIA

Listen and *hear* me. You must go and stop it.

TONY

Then I will.

MARIA [*surprised*]

Can you?

TONY

You don't want even a fist fight? There won't be any fight.

MARIA

I believe you! You *do* have magic.

TONY

Of course, I have you. You go home and dress up. Then tonight, I will come by for you.

MARIA

You cannot come by. My mama . . .

TONY [*after a pause*]

Then I will take you to my house—

MARIA [*shaking her head*]

Your mama . . .

[*Another awkward pause. Then he sees a female dummy and pushes it forward.*]

TONY

She will come running from the kitchen to welcome you. She lives in the kitchen.

MARIA

Dressed so elegant?

TONY

I told her you were coming. She will look at your face and try not to smile. And she will say: Skinny—but pretty.

MARIA

She is plump, no doubt.

TONY [*holding out the waist of dummy's dress*]

Fat!

MARIA [*indicating another female dummy*]

I take after my mama; delicate-boned. [*He kisses her.*] Not in front of Mama! [*He turns the dummy around as she goes to a male dummy.*] Oh, I would like to see Papa in this! Mama will make him ask about your prospects, if you go to church. But Papa—Papa *might* like you.

TONY [*kneeling to the "father" dummy*]

May I have your daughter's hand?

MARIA

He says yes.

TONY

Gracias!

MARIA

And your mama?

TONY

I'm afraid to ask her.

MARIA

Tell her she's not getting a daughter; she's getting rid of a son!

TONY

She says yes.

MARIA

She has good taste. [*She grabs up the wedding veil and puts it on as Tony arranges the dummies.*]

TONY

Maid of honor!

MARIA

That color is bad for Anita.

TONY

Best man!

MARIA

That is my Papa!

TONY

Sorry, Papa. Here we go, Riff: Womb to Tomb! [*He takes hat off dummy.*]

MARIA

Now you see, Anita, I told you there was nothing to worry about.

[*Music starts as she leaves the dummy and walks up to Tony. They look at each other—and the play acting vanishes. Slowly, seriously, they turn front, and together kneel as before an altar.*]

TONY

I, Anton, take thee, Maria . . .

MARIA
I, Maria, take thee, Anton . . .
TONY
For richer, for poorer . . .
MARIA
In sickness and in health . . .
TONY
To love and to honor . . .
MARIA
To hold and to keep . . .
TONY
From each sun to each moon . . .
MARIA
From tomorrow to tomorrow . . .
TONY
From now to forever . . .
MARIA
Till death do us part.
TONY
With this ring, I thee wed.
MARIA
With this ring, I thee wed.
TONY [sings]
Make of our hands one hand,
Make of our hearts one heart,
Make of our vows one last vow:
Only death will part us now.
MARIA
Make of our lives one life,
Day after day, one life.
BOTH
Now it begins, now we start
One hand, one heart—
Even death won't part us now.
[They look at each other, then at the reality of their "game." They smile tenderly, ruefully, and slowly put the dummies back into position. Though brought back to earth, they continue to sing.]
Make of our lives one life,
Day after day, one life.

Now it begins, now we start
One hand, one heart—
Even death won't part us now.

> [*Very gently, he kisses her hand.*]
> *The Lights Fade Out.*

SCENE EIGHT.

6:00 to 9:00 P.M. The neighborhood.

    Spotlights pick out Riff and the Jets, Bernardo and the Sharks, Anita, Maria and Tony against small sets representing different places in the neighborhood. All are waiting expectantly for the coming of night, but for very different reasons.

JETS [*sing*]
The Jets are gonna have their day
Tonight.

SHARKS
The Sharks are gonna have their way
Tonight.

JETS
The Puerto Ricans grumble,
"Fair fight."
But if they start a rumble,
We'll rumble 'em right.

SHARKS
We're gonna hand 'em a surprise
Tonight.

JETS
We're gonna cut 'em down to size
Tonight.

SHARKS
We said, "O.K., no rumpus,
No tricks"—
But just in case they jump us,

We're ready to mix
Tonight!

BOTH GANGS

We're gonna rock it tonight,
We're gonna jazz it up and have us a ball.
They're gonna get it tonight;
The more they turn it on, the harder they'll fall!

JETS

Well, they began it—

SHARKS

Well, they began it—

BOTH GANGS

And we're the ones to stop 'em once and for all,
Tonight!

ANITA

Anita's gonna get her kicks
Tonight.
We'll have our private little mix
Tonight.
He'll walk in hot and tired,
So what?
Don't matter if he's tired,
As long as he's hot
Tonight!

TONY

Tonight, tonight,
Won't be just any night,
Tonight there will be no morning star.

Tonight, tonight,
I'll see my love tonight.
And for us, stars will stop where they are.

Today
The minutes seem like hours,
The hours go so slowly,
And still the sky is light . . .

Oh moon, grow bright,
And make this endless day endless night!

RIFF, [*to Tony*]
I'm counting on you to be there
Tonight.
When Diesel wins it fair and square
Tonight.

That Puerto Rican punk'll
Go down.
And when he's hollered Uncle
We'll tear up the town
Tonight!

MARIA
Tonight, tonight
Won't be just any night . . .
[*She reprises the same chorus Tony has just sung.*]

RIFF
So I can count on you, boy?

TONY
All right.

RIFF
We're gonna have us a ball.

TONY
All right . . .

[*Regretting his impatience.*]

Womb to tomb!

RIFF
Sperm to worm!
I'll see you there about eight . . .

TONY
Tonight . . .

BERNARDO *and* SHARKS
We're gonna rock it tonight!!!

ANITA
Tonight . . .
[*All have been singing at once, reprising the choruses they sang before.*]

BERNARDO *and* SHARKS
We're gonna jazz it tonight
They're gonna get it tonight—tonight.
They began it—they began it

And we're the ones
To stop 'em once and for all!
The Sharks are gonna have their way,
The Sharks are gonna have their day,
We're gonna rock it tonight—
Tonight!

ANITA
Tonight,
Late tonight,
We're gonna mix it tonight.
Anita's gonna have her day,
Anita's gonna have her day,
Bernardo's gonna have his way
Tonight—tonight.
Tonight—this very night,
We're gonna rock it tonight,
Tonight!

RIFF *and* JETS
They began it.
They began it.
We'll stop 'em once and for all
The Jets are gonna have their day,
The Jets are gonna have their way,
We're gonna rock it tonight.
Tonight!

MARIA
Tonight there will be no morning star.
Tonight, tonight, I'll see my love tonight.
When we kiss, stars will stop where they are.

TONY *and* MARIA
Today the minutes seem like hours.
The hours go so slowly,
And still the sky is light.
Oh, moon, grow bright,
And make this endless day endless night,
Tonight!

[*The lights build with the music to the climax, and
then blackout at the final exultant note.*]

SCENE NINE.

9:00 P.M. *Under the highway.*

A dead end: rotting plaster-and-brick walls and mesh wire fences. A street lamp.

It is nightfall. The almost-silhouetted gangs come in from separate sides: climbing over the fences or crawling through holes in the walls. There is silence as they fan out on opposite sides of the cleared space. Then Bernardo and Diesel remove their jackets, handing them to their seconds: Chino and Riff.

BERNARDO

Ready.

CHINO

Ready!

DIESEL

Ready.

RIFF

Ready! Come center and shake hands.

BERNARDO

For what?

RIFF

That's how it's done, buddy boy.

BERNARDO

More gracious living? Look: I don't go for that pretend crap you all go for in this country. Every one of you hates every one of us, and we hate you right back. I don't drink with nobody I hate, I don't shake hands with nobody I hate. Let's get at it.

RIFF

OK.

BERNARDO [*moving toward center*]

Here we go.

[*Diesel begins to move toward him. There are*

encouragements called from each side. The "fair fight" is just beginning when there is an interruption.]

TONY

Hold it! [*He leaps over a fence and starts toward Bernardo.*]

RIFF

Get with the gang.

TONY

No.

RIFF

What're you doin'?

BERNARDO

Maybe he has found the guts to fight his own battles.

TONY [*smiling*]

It doesn't take guts if you *have* a battle. But we haven't got one, 'Nardo. [*He extends his hand for Bernardo to shake it. Bernardo knocks the hand away and gives Tony a shove that sends him sprawling.*]

BERNARDO

Bernardo.

RIFF [*quiet, strong*]

The deal is a fair fight between you and Diesel. [*To Tony, who has gotten up:*] Get with the gang.

[*During the following, Bernardo flicks Tony's shirt, pushes his shoulder, pinches his cheek.*]

BERNARDO [*to Tony*]

I'll give you a battle, Kiddando.

DIESEL

You've got one.

BERNARDO

I'll take pretty boy on as a warm-up. Afraid, pretty boy? Afraid, chicken? Afraid, gutless?

RIFF

Cut that--

TONY

I don't want to, Bernardo ...

BERNARDO

I'm sure.

TONY

Bernardo, you've got it wrong.

BERNARDO

Are you chicken?

TONY

You *won't* understand!

BERNARDO

What d'ya say, chicken?

ACTION

Get him, Tony!

BERNARDO

He *is* chicken.

DIESEL

Tony—

A-RAB

Get him!

TONY

Bernardo, *don't.*

BERNARDO

Don't what, pretty little chicken?

RIFF

Tony, don't just stand—

BERNARDO

Yellow-bellied chicken—

RIFF

TONY!

ACTION

Murder him!

SNOWBOY

Kill him!

TONY

DON'T PUSH ME!

BERNARDO

Come on, you yellow-bellied Polack bas——

[*He never finishes, for Riff hauls off and hits him.
Immediately, the two gangs alert, and the following
action takes on the form of a dance. As Bernardo
reels back to his feet, he reaches for his back
pocket. Riff reaches for his back pocket, and at
the same instant each brings forth a gleaming knife.*

They jockey for position, feinting, dueling; the two
gangs shift position, now and again temporarily
obscuring the fighters. Tony tries to get between
them.]

RIFF

Hold him!

[Diesel and Action grab Tony and hold him back.
The fight continues. Riff loses his knife, is passed
another by a Jet. At last, he has Bernardo in a
position where it seems that he will be able to run
him through. Tony breaks from Diesel and, crying
out, moves to stop Riff.]

TONY

Riff, don't! [*Riff hesitates a moment; the moment is enough*
for Bernado—whose hand goes forward with a driving mo-
tion, running his knife into Riff. Tony leaps forward to
catch Riff. He breaks his fall, then takes the knife from his
hand. A free-for-all has broken out as Tony, Riff's knife in
hand, leaps at the triumphant Bernardo. All this happens
terribly fast; and Tony rams his knife into Bernardo. The
free-for-all continues a moment longer. Then there is a
sharp police whistle. Everything comes to a dead stop—
dead silence. Then a distant police siren: the kids waver,
run one way, another, in panic, confusion. As the stage is
cleared, Tony stands, horrified, over the still bodies of Riff
and Bernardo. He bends over Riff's body; then he rolls
Bernardo's body over—and stares. Then Tony raises his
voice in an anguished cry.]

MARIA!

[Another police whistle, closer now, but he doesn't
move. From the shadows, Anybodys appears. She
scurries to Tony and tugs at his arm. A siren, an-
other whistle, then a searchlight cuts across the
playground. Anybodys' insistent tugging brings Tony
to the realization of the danger. He crouches, starts
to run with her to one escapeway. She reaches it
first, goes out—but the searchlight hits it just as
he would go through. He stops, runs the other way.
He darts here, there, and finally gets away as a dis-
tant clock begins to boom.]   The Curtain Falls

ACT II

SCENE ONE.

9:15 P.M. A bedroom.

Part of a parlor is also visible. The bedroom has a window opening onto the fire escape, a bed on a wall, a small shrine to the Virgin, and a curtained doorway, rear. There is a door between the bedroom and the parlor.

Gay music for Consuelo, who is examining herself in the mirror, and for Rosalia, who is on the bed, finishing her nails.

CONSUELO

This is my last night as a blonde.

ROSALIA

No loss.

CONSUELO

A gain! The fortune teller told Pepe a dark lady was coming into his life.

ROSALIA

So that's why he's not taking you out after the rumble!

[*The music becomes festively, humorously Spanish as Maria enters through the curtained doorway. She is finishing getting very dressed up.*]

MARIA

There is not going to be a rumble.

ROSALIA

Another fortune teller.

CONSUELO

Where is Chino escorting you after the rumble-that-is-not-going-to-be-a-rumble?

MARIA

Chino is escorting me no place.

ROSALIA

She is just dolling up for us. *Gracias, querida.*

MARIA

No, not for you. Can you keep a sec

CONSUELO

I'm hot for secrets!

MARIA

Tonight is my wedding night!

CONSUELO

The poor thing is out of her mind.

MARIA

I am: crazy!

ROSALIA

She might be at that. She looks somehow different.

MARIA

I do?

ROSALIA

And I think she is up to something tonight.

MARIA

I am?

CONSUELO

"I do?" "I am?" What is going on with you?

MARIA [*sings*]

I feel pretty,
Oh, so pretty,
I feel pretty, and witty and bright,
And I pity
Any girl who isn't me tonight.

I feel charming,
Oh, so charming—
It's alarming how charming I feel,
And so pretty
That I hardly can believe I'm real.

See the pretty girl in that mirror there:
Who can that attractive girl be?
    Such a pretty face,
    Such a pretty dress,
    Such a pretty smile,

Such a pretty me!

I feel stunning
And entrancing—
Feel like running and dancing for joy,
For I'm loved
By a pretty wonderful boy!

ROSALIA *and* CONSUELO

Have you met my good friend Maria,
The craziest girl on the block?
You'll know her the minute you see her—
She's the one who is in an advanced state of shock.

She thinks she's in love.
She thinks she's in Spain.
She isn't in love,
She's merely insane.

It must be the heat
Or some rare disease
Or too much to eat,
Or maybe it's fleas.

Keep away from her—
Send for Chino!
This is not the Mar-
Ia we know!

Modest and pure,
Polite and refined,
Well-bred and mature
And out of her mind!

MARIA

I feel pretty,
Oh, so pretty,
That the city should give me its key.
A committee
Should be organized to honor me.

I feel dizzy,

I feel sunny,
I feel fizzy and funny and fine,
And so pretty,
Miss America can just resign!
See the pretty girl in that mirror there:

        ROSALIA *and* CONSUELO
What mirror where?

        MARIA
Who can that attractive girl be?

        ROSALIA *and* CONSUELO
    Which? What? Where? Whom?

        MARIA
    Such a pretty face,
    Such a pretty dress,
    Such a pretty smile,
Such a pretty me!

        ALL
I feel stunning
And entrancing—
Feel like running and dancing for joy,
For I'm loved
By a pretty wonderful boy!

        CHINO [*offstage*]
Maria!

        CONSUELO
It's Chino.

        ROSALIA
The happy bridegroom.

        CHINO [*closer*]
Maria!

        MARIA
Please—

        CONSUELO
Yes, little bride, we're going.

                                        [*She exits.*]

        ROSALIA
They have a quaint old-fashioned custom in this country,
Maria: they get married here *before* the wedding night.
[*She follows Consuelo out as Chino enters from offstage.
His clothes are dirty and torn from the fight; his face is*

*smeared. They shake their heads at him and flounce out.
He closes the outer door.*]

CHINO

Maria? . . .

MARIA

I'm in here. I was just getting ready to—[*She is hurriedly
trying to put a bathrobe over her dress. Chino comes in
before she can finish, so that she leaves it over her shoulders,
holding it closed with her hand.*]

CHINO

Where are your parents?

MARIA

At the store. If I had known you were—You have been
fighting, Chino.

CHINO

Yes. I am sorry.

MARIA

That is not like you.

CHINO

No.

MARIA

Why, Chino?

CHINO

I don't know why. It happened so fast.

MARIA

You must wash up.

CHINO

Maria—

MARIA

You can go in there.

CHINO

In a minute. Maria . . . at the rumble—

MARIA

There was no rumble.

CHINO

There was.

MARIA

You are wrong.

CHINO

No; there was. Nobody meant for it to happen . . .

MARIA

... Tell me.

CHINO

It's bad.

MARIA

Very bad?

CHINO [*nods*]

You see ... [*He moves closer to her, helplessly.*]

MARIA

It will be easier if you say it very fast.

CHINO [*nods*]

There was a fight—[*She nods.*] And 'Nardo—[*She nods.*] And somehow a knife—and 'Nardo and someone—[*He takes her hand.*]

MARIA

Tony. What happened to Tony? [*The name stops Chino. He drops her hand: the robe opens.*] Tell me! [*Crudely, Chino yanks off the robe, revealing that she is dressed to go out.*] Chino, is Tony all right?!

CHINO

He killed your brother. [*He walks into the parlor, slamming the door behind him. A pause.*]

MARIA

You are lying. [*Chino has started to leave the parlor, but turns back now. Swiftly searching behind furniture, he comes up with an object wrapped in material the same color as Bernardo's shirt. From the bedroom, Maria's voice calls out, louder.*] You are lying, Chino! [*Coldly, Chino unwraps a gun, which he puts in his pocket. There is the sound of a police siren at a distance. He goes out. During this, Maria has knelt before the shrine on the wall. She rocks back and forth in prayer, some of it in Spanish, some of it in English.*] Make it not be true ... please make it not be true. ... I will do anything: make *me* die. ... Only, please—make it not be true. [*As she prays, Tony appears at the fire-escape window and quietly climbs in. His shirt is ripped, half-torn off. He stands still, limp, watching her. Aware that someone is in the room, she stops her prayers. Slowly, her head turns; she looks at him for a long moment. Then, almost in one spring, she is on him, her fists beating his chest.*] Killer

killer killer killer killer—[*But her voice breaks with tears, her arms go about him, and she buries her face in his chest, kissing him. She begins to slide down his body. He supports her as, together, they go to the floor, he cradling her body in his arms. He pushes her hair back from her face; kisses her hair, her face, between the words that tumble out.*]

TONY

I tried to stop it; I did try. I don't know how it went wrong. . . . I didn't mean to hurt him; I didn't want to; I didn't know I had. But Riff . . . Riff was like my brother. So when Bernardo killed him—[*She lifts her head.*] 'Nardo didn't mean it, either. Oh, I know he didn't! Oh, no. I didn't come to tell you just for you to forgive me so I could go to the police—

MARIA

No!

TONY

It's easy now—

MARIA

No . . .

TONY

Whatever you want, I'll do—

MARIA

Stay. Stay with me.

TONY

I love you so much.

MARIA

Tighter.

[*Music starts.*]

TONY

We'll be all right. I know it. We're really together now.

MARIA

But it's not us! It's everything around us!

TONY

Then we'll find some place where nothing can get to us; not one of them, not anything. And—

[*He sings:*]

I'll take you away, take you far far away out of here,
Far far away till the walls and the streets disappear,

Somewhere there must be a place we can feel we're free,
Somewhere there's got to be some place for you and for me.

> [*As he sings, the walls of the apartment begin to
> move off, and the city walls surrounding them begin
> to close in on them. Then the apartment itself goes,
> and the two lovers begin to run, battering against
> the walls of the city, beginning to break through as
> chaotic figures of the gangs, of violence, flail around
> them. But they do break through, and suddenly—
> they are in a world of space and air and sun. They
> stop, looking at it, pleased, startled, as boys and
> girls from both sides come on. And they, too, stop
> and stare, happy, pleased. Their clothes are soft
> pastel versions of what they have worn before. They
> begin to dance, to play: no sides, no hostility now;
> just joy and pleasure and warmth. More and more
> join, making a world that Tony and Maria want to
> be in, belong to, share their love with. As they go
> into the steps of a gentle love dance, a voice is
> heard singing.*]

OFFSTAGE VOICE [*sings*]

There's a place for us,
Somewhere a place for us.
Peace and quiet and room and air
Wait for us
Somewhere.

There's a time for us,
Someday a time for us,
Time together with time to spare,
Time to learn, time to care
Someday!

Somewhere
We'll find a new way of living,
We'll find a way of forgiving
Somewhere,
Somewhere . . .

There's a place for us,

A time and place for us.
Hold my hand and we're halfway there.
Hold my hand and I'll take you there
Someday,
Somehow,
Somewhere!

> [*The lovers hold out their hands to each other; the others follow suit: Jets to Sharks; Sharks to Jets. And they form what is almost a procession winding its triumphant way through this would-be world, as they sing the words of the song with wonderment. Then, suddenly, there is a dead stop. The harsh shadows, the fire escapes of the real, tenement world cloud the sky, and the figures of Riff and Bernardo slowly walk on. The dream becomes a nightmare: as the city returns, there are brief reenactments of the knife fight, of the deaths. Maria and Tony are once again separated from each other by the violent warring of the two sides. Maria tries to reach Bernardo, Tony tries to stop Riff; the lovers try to reach each other, but they cannot. Chaotic confusion and blackness, after which they find themselves back in the bedroom, clinging to each other desperately. With a blind refusal to face what they know must be, they reassure each other desperately as they sing.*]

TONY *and* MARIA

Hold my hand and we're halfway there.
Hold my hand and I'll take you there
Someday,
Somehow,
Somewhere!

> [*As the lights fade, together they sink back on the bed.*]

SCENE TWO.

10:00 P.M. *Another alley.*
   A fence with loose boards; angles between buildings.

Softly, from behind the fence, the Jet gang whistle. A pause, then the answering whistle, softly, from offstage or around a corner. Now a loose board flips up and Baby John wriggles through the fence. He whistles again, timidly, and A-rab comes on.

A - R A B

They get you yet?

BABY JOHN

No. You?

A - R A B

Hell, no.

BABY JOHN

You seen Tony?

A - R A B

Nobody has.

BABY JOHN

Geez . . .

A - R A B

You been home yet?

BABY JOHN

Uh uh.

A - R A B

Me, either.

BABY JOHN

Just hidin' around?

A - R A B

Uh huh.

BABY JOHN

A-rab . . . did you get a look at 'em?

A - R A B

Look at who?

Ya know. At the rumble. Riff and Bernardo.   [*Pause.*]

A - R A B

I wish it was yesterday.

BABY JOHN

Wadaya say we run away?

A - R A B

What's a matter? You scared?

BABY JOHN

... Yeah.

A - R A B

You cut it out, ya hear? You're only makin' me scared and that scares me! [*Police whistle. He grabs Baby John.*] Last thing ever is to let a cop know you're scared or anythin'.

KRUPKE [*offstage*]

Hey, you two!

A - R A B

Play it big with the baby blues.

BABY JOHN [*scared*]

OK.

A - R A B [*gripping him*]

Big, not scared, big!

[*Again a whistle. Elaborately casual, they start sauntering off as Krupke appears.*]

KRUPKE

Yeah, you.

[*They stop, so surprised.*]

A - R A B

Why it *is* Officer Krupke, Baby John.

BABY JOHN [*quaking*]

Top of the evening, Officer Krupke.

KRUPKE

I'll crack the top of your skulls if you punks don't stop when I whistle.

A - R A B

But we stopped the very moment we heard.

BABY JOHN

We got twenty-twenty hearing.

KRUPKE

You wanna get hauled down to the station house?

BABY JOHN

Indeed not, sir.

KRUPKE

I'll make a little deal. I know you was rumblin' under the highway—

BABY JOHN

We was at the playground, sir.

A-RAB

We like the playground. It keeps us deprived kids off the foul streets.

BABY JOHN

It gives us comradeship—

A-RAB

A place for pleasant pastimes—And for us, born like we was on the hot pavements—

KRUPKE

OK, wise apples, down to the station house.

BABY JOHN

Which way?

A-RAB

This way! [*He gets down on all fours, Baby John pushes Krupke, so that he tumbles over A-rab. Baby John starts off one way, A-rab the other. Krupke hesitates, then runs after one of them, blowing his whistle like mad. The moment he is off, A-rab and Baby John appear through the fence, followed by the other Jets.*] Look at the brass-ass run!

BABY JOHN

I hope he breaks it!

ACTION

Get the lead out, fat boy!

DIESEL

Easy. He'll come back and drag us down the station house.

ACTION

I already been.

SNOWBOY

We both already been.

A-RAB

What happened?

SNOWBOY

A big fat nuthin'!

A-RAB

How come?

SNOWBOY

Cops believe everythin' they read in the papers.

ACTION

To them we ain't human. We're cruddy juvenile delinquents. So that's what we give 'em.

SNOWBOY [*imitating Krupke*]

Hey, you!

ACTION

Me, Officer Krupke?

SNOWBOY

Yeah, you! Gimme one good reason for not draggin' ya
down the station house, ya punk.

ACTION [*sings*]

Dear kindly Sergeant Krupke,
You gotta understand—
It's just our bringin' upke
That gets us out of hand.
Our mothers all are junkies,
Our fathers all are drunks.

ALL

Golly Moses—natcherly we're punks!

Gee, Officer Krupke, we're very upset;
We never had the love that every child oughta get.
We ain't no delinquents,
We're misunderstood.
Deep down inside us there is good!

ACTION

There is good!

ALL

There is good, there is good,
There is untapped good.
Like inside, the worst of us is good.

SNOWBOY [*imitating Krupke*]

That's a touchin' good story.

ACTION

Lemme tell it to the world!

SNOWBOY [*imitating Krupke*]

Just tell it to the judge.

ACTION [*to Diesel*]

Dear kindly Judge, your Honor,
My parents treat me rough.
With all their marijuana,
They won't give me a puff.
They didn't wanna have me,

But somehow I was had.
Leapin' lizards—that's why I'm so bad!

DIESEL [*imitating a judge*]

Right!
Officer Krupke, you're really a square;
This boy don't need a judge, he needs a analyst's care!
It's just his neurosis that oughta be curbed—
He's psychologically disturbed!

ACTION

I'm disturbed!

ALL

We're disturbed, we're disturbed,
We're the most disturbed.
Like we're psychologically disturbed.

DIESEL [*speaks, still acting part of judge*]

Hear ye, Hear ye! In the opinion of this court, this child is depraved on account he ain't had a normal home.

ACTION

Hey. I'm depraved on account I'm deprived!

DIESEL [*as judge*]

So take him to a headshrinker.

ACTION [*to A-rab*]

My father is a bastard,
My ma's an S.O.B.
My grandpa's always plastered,
My grandma pushes tea.
My sister wears a mustache,
My brother wears a dress.
Goodness gracious, that's why I'm a mess!

A-RAB [*as psychiatrist*]

Yes!
Officer Krupke, you're really a slob.
This boy don't need a doctor, just a good honest job.
Society's played him a terrible trick,
And sociologically he's sick!

ACTION

I am sick!

ALL

We are sick, we are sick,
We are sick sick sick,

Like we're sociologically sick!

      A - R A B [*speaks as psychiatrist*]

In my opinion, this child don't need to have his head shrunk
at all. Juvenile delinquency is purely a social disease.

      A C T I O N

Hey, I got a social disease!

      A - R A B [*as psychiatrist*]

So take him to a social worker!

      A C T I O N [*to Baby John*]

Dear kindly social worker,
They say go earn a buck,
Like be a soda jerker,
Which means like be a schmuck.
It's not I'm antisocial,
I'm only antiwork.
Glory Osky, that's why I'm a jerk!

      B A B Y   J O H N [*as female social worker*]

Eek!
Officer Krupke, you've done it again.
This boy don't need a job, he needs a year in the pen.
It ain't just a question of misunderstood;
Deep down inside him, he's no good!

      A C T I O N

I'm no good!

      A L L

We're no good, we're no good,
We're no earthly good,
Like the best of us is no damn good!

      D I E S E L [*as judge*]

The trouble is he's crazy,

      A - R A B [*as psychiatrist*]

The trouble is he drinks.

      B A B Y   J O H N [*as social worker*]

The trouble is he's lazy.

      D I E S E L [*as judge*]

The trouble is he stinks.

      A - R A B [*as psychiatrist*]

The trouble is he's growing.

      B A B Y   J O H N [*as social worker*]

The trouble is he's grown!

ALL

Krupke, we got troubles of our own!

Gee, Officer Krupke,

We're down on our knees,

'Cause no one wants a fella with a social disease.

Gee, Officer Krupke,

What are we to do?

Gee, Officer Krupke—

Krup you!

> [*At the end of the song, Anybodys appears over the fence.*]

ANYBODYS

Buddy boys!

ACTION

Ah! Go wear a skirt.

ANYBODYS

I got scabby knees. Listen—

ACTION [*to the gang*]

Come on, we gotta make sure those PRs know we're on top.

DIESEL

Geez, Action, ain't we had enough?

ANYBODYS [*going after them*]

Wotta buncha Old Man Rivers: they don't know nothin'
and they don't say nuthin'.

ACTION

Diesel, the question ain't whether we had enough—

ANYBODYS

The question is: Where's Tony and what party is lookin'
for him.

ACTION

What do you know?

ANYBODYS

I know I gotta get a skirt. [*She starts off, but Diesel stops her.*]

DIESEL

Come on, Anybodys, tell me.

SNOWBOY

Ah, what's that freak know?

ANYBODYS

Plenty. I figgered somebody oughta infiltrate PR territory

and spy around. I'm very big with shadows, ya know. I can slip in and out of 'em like wind through a fence.

SNOWBOY

Boy, is she ever makin' the most of it!

ANYBODYS

You bet your fat A, I am!

ACTION

Go on. Wadd'ya hear?

ANYBODYS

I heard Chino tellin' the Sharks somethin' about Tony and Bernardo's sister. And then Chino said, "If it's the last thing I do, I'm going to get Tony."

ACTION

What'd I tell ya? Them PRs won't stop!

SNOWBOY

Easy, Action!

DIESEL

It's bad enough now—

BABY JOHN

Yeah!

ACTION

You forgettin'? Tony came through for us Jets. We gotta find him and protect him from Chino.

A-RAB

Right!

ACTION

OK then! Snowboy—cover the river! [*Snowboy runs off.*] A-rab—get over to Doc's.

BABY JOHN

I'll take the back alleys.

ACTION

Diesel?

DIESEL

I'll cover the park.

ACTION

Good boy! [*He begins to run off.*]

ANYBODYS

What about me?

ACTION

You? You get a hold of the girls and send 'em out as liaison runners so we'll know who's found Tony where.

ANYBODYS

Right! [*She starts to run off.*]

ACTION

Hey! [*She stops.*] You done good, buddy boy.

ANYBODYS [*she has fallen in love*]

Thanks, Daddy-o.

> [*They both run off.*]
> *The Lights Black Out*

SCENE THREE.

11:30 P.M. The bedroom.

The light is, at first, a vague glow on the lovers, who are asleep on the bed. From offstage, faint at first, there is the sound of knocking. It gets louder; Tony stirs. At a distance a police siren sounds, and the knocking is now very loud. Tony bolts upright. Anita comes in from outside and goes to the bedroom door—which is locked—tries the knob.

ANITA [*holding back tears*]

Maria? . . . Maria? [*Tony is reaching for his shirt when Maria sits up. Quickly, he puts his hand, then his lips, on her lips.*] Maria, it's Anita. Why are you locked in?

MARIA

I didn't know it was locked.

ANITA

Open the door. I need you.

> [*Maria reaches for the knob, Tony stops her.*]

MARIA [*a whisper*]

Now you are afraid, too.

ANITA

What?

MARIA [*loud*]

One moment.

TONY [*whispering*]

Doc'll help. I'll get money from him. You meet me at his drugstore.

> [*In the other room, Anita is aware of voices but unsure of what they are saying.*]

At Doc's yes. [*Aloud.*] Coming, Anita!

TONY [*kisses her*]

Hurry!

> [*He scrambles out the window as Maria hastily puts a bathrobe on over her slip. In the other room Anita has stiffened and moved away from the door. She stands staring at it coldly as Maria prattles to her through the door.*]

MARIA

Did you see Chino? He was here before, but he left so angry I think maybe he . . . [*She opens the door and sees Anita's look. A moment, then Anita pushes her aside: looks at the bed, at the window, then turns accusingly to Maria.*] All right: now you know.

ANITA [*savagely*]

And you still don't know: *Tony is one of them!*

> [*She sings bitterly:*]

A boy like that who'd kill your brother,
Forget that boy and find another!
One of your own kind—
Stick to your own kind!

A boy like that will give you sorrow—
You'll meet another boy tomorrow!
One of your own kind,
Stick to your own kind!

A boy who kills cannot love,
A boy who kills has no heart.
And he's the boy who gets your love
And gets your heart—
Very smart, Maria, very smart!

A boy like that wants one thing only,
And when he's done he'll leave you lonely.

He'll murder your love; he murdered mine.
Just wait and see—
Just wait, Maria,
Just wait and see!

MARIA [*sings*]
Oh no, Anita, no—
Anita, no!
It isn't true, not for me,
It's true for you, not for me,
I hear your words—
And in my head
I know they're smart,
But my heart, Anita,
But my heart
Knows they're wrong.
        [*Anita reprises the chorus she has just sung, as Maria
        continues her song.*]
And my heart
Is too strong,
For I belong
To him alone, to him alone,
One thing I know:
I am his,
I don't care what he is.
I don't know why it's so,
I don't want to know.
Oh no, Anita, no—you should know better!
You were in love—or so you said.
You should know better . . .

I have a love, and it's all that I have.
Right or wrong, what else can I do?
I love him; I'm his,
And everything he is
I am, too.
I have a love and it's all that I need,
Right or wrong, and he needs me too.
I love him, we're one;

There's nothing to be done,
Not a thing I can do
But hold him, hold him forever,
Be with him now, tomorrow
And all of my life!

BOTH

When love comes so strong,
There is no right or wrong,
Your love is your life!

ANITA [*quietly*]

Chino has a gun . . . He is sending the boys out to hunt
for Tony—

MARIA [*tears off her bathrobe*]

If he hurts Tony—If he touches him—I swear to you, I'll—

ANITA [*sharply*]

You'll do what Tony did to Bernardo?

MARIA

I love Tony.

ANITA

I know. I loved Bernardo.

[*Schrank comes into the outer room.*]

SCHRANK

Anybody home? [*Goes to bedroom door, Pleasantly.*]
Sorry to disturb you. Guess you're disturbed enough.

MARIA [*gathering her robe*]

Yes. You will excuse me, please. I must go to my brother.

SCHRANK

There are just a coupla questions—

MARIA

Afterwards, please. Later.

SCHRANK

It'll only take a minute.

ANITA

Couldn't you wait until—

SCHRANK [*sharply*]

No! [*A smile to Maria.*] You were at the dance at the gym
last night.

MARIA

Yes.

SCHRANK

Your brother got in a heavy argument because you danced with the wrong boy.

MARIA

Oh?

SCHRANK

Who was the boy?

MARIA

Excuse me. Anita, my head is worse. Will you go to the drugstore and tell them what I need?

SCHRANK

Don't you keep aspirin around?

MARIA

This is something special. Will you go for me, Anita?

ANITA [*hesitates, looks at Maria, then nods*]

Shall I tell him to hold it for you till you come?

MARIA [*to Shrank*]

Will I be long?

SCHRANK

As long as it takes.

MARIA [*to Anita*]

Yes. Tell him I will pick it up myself. [*Anita goes out.*] I'm sorry. Now you asked?

SCHRANK [*as the lights dim*]

I didn't ask, I told you. There was an argument over a boy. Who was that boy?

MARIA

Another from my country.

SCHRANK

And his name?

MARIA

José.

The Lights Are Out

SCENE FOUR.

11:40 P.M. The drugstore.

A-rab and some of the Jets are there as Anybodys and other Jets run in.

ACTION

Where's Tony?

A-RAB

Down in the cellar with Doc.

DIESEL

Ya warn him about Chino?

A-RAB

Doc said he'd tell him.

BABY JOHN

What's he hidin' in the cellar from?

SNOWBOY

Maybe he can't run as fast as you.

ACTION

Cut the frabbajabba.

ANYBODYS

Yeah! The cops'll get hip, if Chino and the PRs don't.

ACTION

Grab some readin' matter; play the juke. Some of ya get outside and if ya see Chino or any PR—

[*The shop doorbell tinkles as Anita enters. Cold silence, then slowly she comes down to the counter. They all stare at her. A long moment. Someone turns on the jukebox; a mambo comes on softly.*]

ANITA

I'd like to see Doc.

ACTION

He ain't here.

ANITA

Where is he?

A-RAB

He's gone to the bank. There was an error in his favor.

ANITA

The banks are closed at night. Where is he?

A-RAB

You know how skinny Doc is. He slipped in through the night-deposit slot.

ANYBODYS

And got stuck halfway in.

ACTION

Which indicates there's no tellin' when he'll be back. *Buenas noches, señorita.*

[*Anita starts to go toward the cellar door.*]

DIESEL

Where you goin'?

ANITA

Downstairs—to see Doc.

ACTION

Didn't I tell ya he ain't here?

ANITA

I'd like to see for myself.

ACTION [*nastily*]

Please.

ANITA [*controlling herself*]

... Please.

ACTION

Por favor.

ANITA

Will you let me pass?

SNOWBOY

She's too dark to pass.

ANITA [*low*]

Don't.

ACTION

Please don't.

SNOWBOY

Por favor.

DIESEL

Non comprende.

A-RAB

Gracias.

BABY JOHN

Di nada.

ANYBODYS

Ai! Mambo! Ai!

ANITA

Listen, you—[*She controls herself.*]

ACTION

We're listenin'.

ANITA

I've got to give a friend of yours a message. I've got to tell
Tony—

DIESEL

He ain't here.

ANITA

I know he is.

ACTION

Who says he is?

A-RAB

Who's the message from?

ANITA

Never mind.

ACTION

Couldn't be from Chino, could it?

ANITA

I want to stop Chino! I want to help!

ANYBODYS

Bernardo's girl wants ta help?

ACTION

Even a greaseball's got feelings.

ANYBODYS

But she wants to help get Tony!

ANITA

No!

ACTION

Not much—Bernardo's tramp!

SNOWBOY

Bernardo's pig!

ACTION

Ya lyin' Spic—!

ANITA

Don't do that!

BABY JOHN

Gold tooth!

DIESEL

Pierced ear!

A-RAB

Garlic mouth!

ACTION

Spic! Lyin' Spic!

[*The taunting breaks out into a wild, savage dance, with epithets hurled at Anita, who is encircled and driven by the whole pack. At the peak, she is shoved so that she falls in a corner. Baby John is lifted up high and dropped on her as Doc enters from the cellar door and yells.*]

DOC

Stop it! . . . What've you been doing now?

[*Dead silence. Anita gets up and looks at them.*]

ANITA [*trying not to cry*]

Bernardo was right . . . If one of you was bleeding in the street, I'd walk by and spit on you. [*She flicks herself off and makes her way toward the door.*]

ACTION

Don't let her go!

DIESEL

She'll tell Chino that Tony—

[*Snowboy grabs her; she shakes loose.*]

ANITA

Let go! [*Facing them.*] I'll give you a message for your American buddy! Tell the murderer Maria's *never* going to meet him! Tell him Chino found out and—and shot her! [*She slams out. There is a stunned silence.*]

DOC

What does it take to get through to you? When do you stop? *You make this world lousy!*

ACTION

That's the way we found it, Doc.

DOC

Get out of here!

[*Slowly, they start to file out.*]
The Lights Fade

SCENE FIVE.

11:50 P.M. The cellar.

Cramped: a box or crate; stairs leading to the drugstore above; a door to the outside.

Tony is sitting on a crate, whistling "Maria" as Doc comes down the stairs, some bills in his hand.

TONY

Make a big sale?

DOC

No.

TONY [*taking the money that Doc is holding*]

Thanks. I'll pay you back as soon as I can.

DOC

Forget that.

TONY

I won't; I couldn't. Doc, you know what we're going to do in the country, Maria and me? We're going to have kids and we'll name them all after you, even the girls. Then when you come to visit—

DOC [*slapping him*]

Wake up! [*Raging.*] Is that the only way to get through to you? Do just what you all do? Bust like a hot-water pipe?

TONY

Doc, what's gotten—

DOC [*overriding angrily*]

Why do you live like there's a war on? [*Low.*] Why do you kill?

TONY

I told you how it happened, Doc. Maria understands. Why can't you?

DOC

I never had a Maria.

TONY [*gently*]

I have, and I'll tell you one thing, Doc. Even if it only lasts from one night to the next, it's worth the world.

DOC

That's all it did last.

TONY

What?

DOC

That was no customer upstairs, just now. That was Anita. [*Pause.*] Maria is dead. Chino found out about you and her—and shot her.

> [*A brief moment. Tony looks at Doc, stunned, numb. He shakes his head, as though he cannot believe this. Doc holds out his hands to him, but Tony backs away, then suddenly turns and runs out the door. As he does, the set flies away and the stage goes dark. In the darkness, we hear Tony's voice.*]

TONY

Chino? *Chino?* Come and get me, too, Chino.

SCENE SIX.

Midnight. The street.

The lights come up to reveal the same set we saw at the beginning of Act One—but it is now jagged with shadows. Tony stands in the emptiness, calling, whirling around as a figure darts out of the shadows and then runs off again.

TONY

Chino? . . . COME ON: GET ME, TOO!

ANYBODYS [*a whisper from the dark*]

Tony . . .

TONY [*swings around*]

Who's that?

ANYBODYS [*darting on*]

Me: Anybodys.

TONY

Get outa here. HEY, CHINO! COME GET ME, DAMN
YOU!

ANYBODYS

What're you doin', Tony?

TONY

I said get outa here! CHINO!

ANYBODYS

Look, maybe if you and me just—

TONY [*savagely*]

It's not playing any more! Can't any of you get that?

ANYBODYS

But the gang—

TONY

You're a girl: *be a girl!* Beat it. [*She retreats.*] CHINO,
I'M CALLING FOR YOU, CHINO! HURRY! IT'S
CLEAR NOW. THERE'S NOBODY BUT ME. COME
ON! Will you, please. I'm waiting for you. I want you to—
[*Suddenly, all the way across the stage from him, a figure
steps out of the dark. He stops and peers as light starts to
glow on it. He utters an unbelieving whisper.*] Maria . . .
Maria?

MARIA

Tony . . . [*As she holds out her arms toward him, another
figure appears: Chino.*]

TONY

MARIA! [*As they run to each other, there is a gun shot.
Tony stumbles, as though he has tripped. Maria catches him
and cradles him in her arms as he falters to the ground.
During this Baby John and A-rab run on; then Pepe and
Indio and other Sharks. Chino stands very still, bewildered
by the gun dangling from his hand. More Jets and Sharks,
some girls run on, and Doc comes out to stare with them.*]
I didn't believe hard enough.

MARIA

Loving is enough.

TONY

Not here. They won't let us be.

MARIA

Then we'll get away.

TONY

Yes, we can. We will. [*He shivers, as though a pain went through him. She holds him closer and begins to sing— without orchestra.*]

MARIA

Hold my hand and we're halfway there.
Hold my hand and I'll take you there,
Someday,
Somehow . . .

[*He has started to join in on the second line. She sings harder, as though to urge him back to life, but his voice falters and he barely finishes the line. She sings on, a phrase or two more, then stops, his body quiet in her arms. A moment, and then, as she gently rests Tony on the floor, the orchestra finishes the last bars of the song. Lightly, she brushes Tony's lips with her fingers. Behind her, Action, in front of a group of Jets, moves to lead them toward Chino. Maria speaks, her voice cold, sharp.*]

Stay back. [*The shawl she has had around her shoulders slips to the ground as she gets up, walks to Chino and holds out her hand. He hands her the gun. She speaks again, in a flat, hard voice.*] How do you fire this gun, Chino? Just by pulling this little trigger? [*She points it at him suddenly; he draws back. She has all of them in front of her now, as she holds the gun out and her voice gets stronger with anger and savage rage.*] How many bullets are left, Chino? Enough for you? [*Pointing at another.*] And you? [*At Action.*] All of you? WE ALL KILLED HIM; and my brother and Riff. I, too. I CAN KILL NOW BECAUSE *I* HATE NOW. [*She has been pointing the gun wildly, and they have all been drawing back. Now, again, she holds it straight out at Action.*] How many can I kill, Chino? How many—and still have one bullet left for me? [*Both hands on the gun, she pushes it forward at Action. But she cannot fire, and she breaks into tears, hurls the gun away and sinks to the ground. Schrank walks on, looks around and starts toward Tony's body. Like a madwoman, Maria races to the body and puts her arms around it, all-embracing, protecting, as she cries out.*] DON'T YOU TOUCH HIM! [*Schrank steps back. Krupke and Glad Hand have appeared in the shadows behind him. Maria now turns and looks at Chino, holds her hand out to him. Slowly he comes and stands by the body. Now she looks at Action, holds out her hand to him. He, too, comes forward, with Diesel, to stand by the body. Pepe joins Chino. Then Maria leans low over Tony's face. Softly, privately.*] Te adoro, Anton.

> [*She kisses him gently. Music starts as the two Jets and two Sharks lift up Tony's body and start to carry him out. The others, boys and girls, fall in behind to make a procession, the same procession they made in the dream ballet, as Baby John comes forward to pick up Maria's shawl and put it over her head. She sits quietly, like a woman in mourning, as the music builds, the lights start to come up and the procession makes its way across the stage. At last, she gets up and, despite the tears on her face, lifts her head proudly, and triumphantly turns to follow the others. The adults—Doc, Schrank, Krupke, Glad Hand—are left bowed, alone, useless.*]
>
> The Curtain Falls

NOTES TO "ROMEO AND JULIET"

Prologue: Enter Chorus. Many Elizabethan dramatists used a chorus as a sort of narrator for the play. The idea was based on the choruses from the classical Greek drama. The Greek chorus, however, was much more complicated, and involved many people. In his later plays, Shakespeare abandoned the practice of using a chorus.

4 *civil blood makes civil hands unclean:* civil in the sense of "civil war": Citizens make their hands unclean by spilling the blood of fellow citizens.

6 *star-crossed:* Star-crossed lovers were lovers born under an unfavorable star, hence destined to destruction. The play contains many references to destiny, fate, and the stars. Generally, Elizabethans believed that heavenly bodies could influence the lives of men. Most of them also believed in the idea of Divine Providence guiding men. Many were able to reconcile the two beliefs.

9 *passage:* progress.

12 *two hours' traffic of our stage:* Shakespeare's plays must have been acted at a very rapid pace. The almost bare, open, outdoor stage and the continuous flow of action, as well as the rapid delivery of lines contributed to the speed of playing.

ACT ONE, SCENE ONE

2 *carry coals:* A coal hauler was one of the dirtiest and lowest of professions; hence a man who carried coals was one who put up with all kinds of insults.

3 *colliers:* coal carriers, who were regarded as shiftless workers or cheats.

4 *an:* if; *choler:* anger.

5 *collar:* a halter or hangman's noose.

2-5 *coals . . . colliers . . . choler . . . collar:* These four words comprise the first play on words, or pun, in the play, which abounds in such puns. To fully appreciate the pun, it is necessary to pronounce "coals" as the Elizabethans did, as though it were "cowls." The pun runs thus: ". . . we'll not carry coals [bear insults] . . . we should be colliers [lazy cheats] . . . I mean be in choler [anger] . . . draw your neck out of the collar [noose]."

10-11 *moves . . . to move:* "moves" (to incite) played off against "to move" (run).

15 *take the wall:* take the position farthest from the street, an act of discourtesy. Even today when a man and woman walk down the street, the man gives the woman, as a matter of courtesy, the position next to the wall. In Shakespeare's day any person of rank or dignity was always given this position. The custom probably grew out of the fact that streets were muddy and often contained drainage ditches down their center. The person who took the wall was protected from unpleasant splashing.

17-18 *The weakest goes to the wall:* from an old proverb meaning "the weakest is shoved to the rear." Again note Gregory's pun.

37 *Poor-John:* salted and dried fish (hake). It was considered dull food; *tool:* sword, but also a pun on the masculine genital organ. Gregory puns here to top Sampson's vulgar bragging about his prowess as a fighter and as a seducer of women. This play has many phrases with two or more meanings that are often bawdy or obscene.

43 *fear:* mistrust.

44 *marry:* indeed; originally an oath, "By the Virgin Mary." *I fear thee:* I have no faith in you. Gregory is not at all sure that Sampson will not run when the fighting starts.

45 *take the law:* Much as is the case today, the one starting the fight was considered wrong. The other could claim self-defense.

47 *list:* please.

49 *bite my thumb:* an insulting gesture similar to the present day "thumbing your nose". The gesture was made by placing the thumbnail under the teeth.

61 *I am for you:* I'm your match or I'm ready to fight you.

65 *Say better; here comes one of my master's kinsmen.* Gregory sees Tybalt approaching and grows bold.

70 *swashing:* slashing, swaggering.

73 *heartless hinds:* weak-spirited servants. Tybalt puns on the hart and the hind, the male and female red deer.

79 *Have at thee:* I shall attack; be on guard.

80 *Clubs, bills, and partisans:* a rallying cry for help in the Elizabethan streets. The clubs were carried by apprentices. Military men and the watch would carry bills and partisans, both of which were kinds of long spears with a cutting edge.

82 *long sword:* Prominent citizens often carried short swords for dress or ceremony. Servants would accompany them with their long swords, which they used in fights. Most young men of Shakespeare's day had abandoned the long sword for the rapier.

83 *A crutch:* A crutch would be better for a man your age.

85 *spite:* to spite me; in defiance of me.

89 *neighbor-stained steel:* steel, or sword, stained with neighbor's blood.

94 *mistempered:* ill-used, with a pun on the tempering of steel.

102 *Cankered . . . cankered:* Again a pun. The first "cankered" is "rusted"; the second is "malignant" or "rankling."

104 *forfeit:* penalty for breaking the peace.

109 *Freetown:* Shakespeare took the basis of his story from a poem by Arthur Brooke, called *Romeus and Juliet.* In that poem the house of the Capulets is called Freetown, Brooke's translation of the Italian *Villa Blanca.*

111 *Who set this ancient quarrel new abroach:* Who gave this old fight a new start?

119 *nothing hurt withal:* not at all hurt by this.

121 *part and part:* either side.

127 *drave:* drove.

128 *sycamore:* a tree symbolic of unhappy lovers.

131 *ware:* aware, wary.

132 *covert:* a hidden place in the woods, such as a thicket.

133 *affections:* feelings.

134 *Which . . . found:* Benvolio says that he too sought to be alone at that time.

135 *humour:* desire, inclination.

142 *Aurora's:* Aurora is the goddess of dawn; hence Romeo has stayed out till dawn.

143 *heavy:* unhappy, as we still use the word in "heavy heart."

147 *humour:* Here the word has more the sense of "mood." Actually physicians of the Middle Ages believed that four fluids, or humours, made up the human body and mind. An improper balance of these fluids caused mental and physical illness.

151 *importuned:* asked repeatedly or begged. The line means, "Have you begged an explanation of him in any way?"

153 *affections' counsellor:* feelings' adviser. In other words, Romeo kept his feelings to himself.

155 *close:* secret. He was close-mouthed.

156 *sounding:* investigation. We still use the phrase, "sound the depths."

157 *envious:* malicious or hateful.

158 *he:* it.

161 *We . . . know:* We are as eager to help him as we are to know what's wrong.

163 *much denied:* greatly refused. "He'll have to refuse me many times before I quit."

164 *happy by thy stay:* lucky in your waiting.

165 *shrift:* confession, especially as one confesses to a priest.

166 *morrow:* morning; *cousin:* term used for any relation other than immediate family; hence Romeo and Benvolio are kinsmen.

175 *view:* appearance.

176 *in proof:* in fact or action.

177 *whose view is muffled still:* whose sight is covered always. Love, or Cupid, was often depicted as wearing a blindfold. Even today we still use the expression, "Love is blind."

178 *will:* desire, i.e., lovemaking.

177–82 This speech contains many couplings of contradictory terms, or paradoxes; e.g., brawling love, loving hate, heavy lightness, serious vanity, cold fire, etc. The technical name for this figure of speech is oxymoron. By use of such figures, Romeo expresses his recognition of the contradictory elements that exist in love and the confusion these elements present to the lover. The signs of the fight remind him that love and hate are opposites of the same drive.

191 *transgression:* offense or crime.

193 *propagate:* increase; *pressed:* oppressed or burdened.

196 *fume:* mist.

197 *Being purged:* Being cleared of smoke and mist.

202 *Soft:* Wait.

205 *sadness:* seriousness.

207 *sadly:* seriously.

209 *ill urged:* badly advised. It is not a good idea to talk to a sick man about making his will.

212 *mark-man:* a pun: "marksman" and "point, man."

213 *fair:* clear. Here the pun is on the previous line's *fair*, meaning "beautiful."

215 *Dian's wit:* Diana was the goddess of chastity. Rosaline had her wit, or intelligence, in defending her virtue.

216 *proof:* tested armor.

218 *stay:* heed.

220 *ope her lap to saint-seducing gold:* In Greek mythology, Danae, the mother of Perseus, was seduced by Zeus in the form of a shower of gold.

223 *still:* always.

225 *starved:* starved to death.

227–8 *wisely too fair . . . despair:* She is too fair (honorable) to earn heaven by making me lose hope (despair). But this, of course, is what Rosaline has done. In modern terms the phrase is something like this: She is too good to do this to me.

235 *to call . . . question more:* "to call in question" is "to examine" or "consider"; hence, when Benvolio tells Romeo to examine other beauties, Romeo says that this is simply a way of examining Rosaline's beauty the more, implying that the others would merely suffer in comparison.

236–7 *These happy masks . . . hide the fair:* These fortunate masks that hide ladies' faces remind us of the beauty hidden below them. In Shakespeare's day ladies wore masks to many public functions. This habit was inspired by more than a sense of discretion. The ladies admired a pale or ivory complexion, and the masks, usually black, protected their faces from the sun.

242 *who passed that passing fair:* again a play on words. "Passed" means "surpassed." "Passing" means "exceedingly."

244 *I'll pay . . . in debt:* I'll teach you to forget or else die in the attempt.

ACT ONE, SCENE TWO

1 *bound:* obliged (to keep the peace).

4 *reckoning:* reputation.

8 *yet a stranger in the world:* still young. Capulet states this, but then goes right ahead and arranges the marriage. Perhaps he is merely going through the formality of being reluctant, or, perhaps, he talks himself into the whole thing in his next speech.

9 *fourteen years:* In Brooke's poem, Juliet is sixteen. In the earlier Italian sources, she is eighteen. Shakespeare may have been influenced by a contemporary play, Marlowe's *Jew of Malta*, in which the heroine is fourteen.

13 *marred:* An old proverb ran, "The maid that soon married is, soon marred is."

14 *Earth . . . but she:* His other children are dead and buried.

15 *hopeful lady:* the only woman who can carry on my posterity.

17 *My will to her consent is but a part:* I only agree if she does. This statement is either a mere formality or Capulet deceives himself. He later shows that he has no intention of giving Juliet a chance to say no.

19 *fair according voice:* happily agreeing voice.

30 *Inherit:* Possess.

32–3 *Which . . . none:* This is a difficult line, and scholars do not agree as to its meaning. Some maintain that Capulet is bragging about his daughter. A better reading seems to be, "Look all the ladies over. My daughter may be counted among them as one of them, but has no reputation for beauty." He is punning on the proverb, "One is no number." Capulet seems to be displaying a false modesty about Juliet's beauty.

34 *sirrah:* term of address to a servant or person of inferior rank.

37 *stay:* wait upon.

39–41 *shoemaker . . . nets:* The servant confuses four old proverbs; one, for example, is, "The shoemaker should stick to his last."

45 *in good time:* He sees Romeo and Benvolio approach.

48 *holp:* helped.

51 *rank:* corrupt.

52 *plantain leaf:* the leaf of a plant used for medicinal purposes. It was considered especially good for bruises or for stopping the flow of blood.

57 *God-den:* good evening.

65 *rest you merry:* may you remain happy, an expression similar to our "so long." Obviously the servant is confused by Romeo and thinks he cannot read.

85–6 *crush a cup of wine:* drink a cup of wine. This is a slang phrase akin to our "crack a bottle."

87 *ancient:* old, in the sense of long established.

90 *unattainted:* impartial.

95 *these:* these eyes.

96 *Transparent heretics:* Obvious disbelievers. Romeo holds Rosaline's beauty to be the religion of his eyes and that, if those eyes saw equal beauty, they would be heretics to their faith in Rosaline.

100 *poised:* weighed or balanced.
104 *scant:* scarcely.
106 *of mine own:* of my own love, i.e., Rosaline.

ACT ONE, SCENE THREE

2 *What:* An exclamation used in calling, such as "oh."
God forbid: that anything is wrong, since she does not answer.
Another possible explanation of the line is that a lady-bird,
though a term of endearment, is also a term for a tart. Hence
the Nurse, realizing the double meaning, says, "God forbid."

6 *give leave awhile:* leave us alone awhile.

9 *Thou's:* Thou shalt.

10 *a pretty age:* a fitting age to discuss marriage.

12 *lay:* bet. We still use the term in this sense today; *teen:*
sorrow.

14 *Lammas-tide:* August 1, the feast of the first fruits and
the hottest season of the year. In Brooke's poem, the incident
took place on Easter Sunday.

22 *marry:* indeed. See Scene one, line 44.

29 *I do bear a brain:* I've got a head on my shoulders.

31 *fool:* affectionate term like "foolish darling."

32 *techy:* irritable or peevish.

33–4 *Shake . . . trudge:* When the quake hit, the dove-house
began to shake and it was a sigh as though it had said to the
Nurse "shake a leg" or "get moving." She says there was no
need to tell her to get moving (*trudge*). *trow:* think, guess.

36 *high-lone:* all alone; *by th' rood:* by the cross, a mild
oath.

38 *broke her brow:* cut her forehead.

40 *'A:* he.

43 *by my holidame:* originally a "halidom," a holy relic, on
which an oath was taken. Afterward it became confused with
the Virgin Mary, holy dame.

48 *stinted:* stopped.

53 *young cockerel's stone:* young rooster's testicle.

59 *mark thee to:* mark you out for or select you for.

72 *much upon these years:* at about the same age.

76 *why he's a man of wax:* a perfect specimen, as though an
artist modeled him in wax.

83 *married lineament:* harmonizing feature.

84 *one another lends content:* each feature sets off the other.

85 *what obscured in that fair volume lies:* what is not seen
in that beautiful face.

86 *margent:* margin. It was customary at that time for scholars to explain the meaning of a text in the margin of a book. This technique is still used on an informal basis today, but for formal comment we use footnotes. The figure of speech could be translated, "What you don't find in the volume of his face, look for in the footnotes of his eyes."

88 *cover:* the cover of the beautiful book that is Paris. As a wife Juliet would complete his beauty and enfold him in her caresses.

89–90 *The fish . . . to hide:* Here Lady Capulet continues the figure of speech of Paris as a book, but she also puns on the word "fish." There is a fish in the sea, Juliet, who will cover his handsome book with her beautiful appearance. Fishskins were used as book covers in those days.

97 *I'll look to like, if looking liking move:* I'll look at him and like him, if looking will make me like him.

101–2 *nurse cursed in the pantry:* they were angry with her in the kitchen because she was not there to help.

103 *straight:* immediately.

ACT ONE, SCENE FOUR

1 *What, shall . . . without apology?:* Romeo and his friends are in costume and masks in preparation for "crashing" the Capulet ball. It was customary for such groups of revelers to have someone make a speech of dedication as a reason or excuse for their appearance. Romeo asks if they should observe this custom or go on without a formal reason (*apology*).

3 *prolixity:* wordiness. "Such wordiness is old-fashioned."

4 *Cupid hoodwinked:* Cupid blindfolded. The speech might be given by someone so costumed.

5 *Tartar's painted bow of lath:* an imitation Tartar's bow.

6 *crow-keeper:* a young boy in the fields who acted as a scarecrow. He carried a bow and arrow.

7–8 *without-book . . . prompter:* an introductory speech that is not properly memorized from the book but is spoken by an actor, without confidence, as the prompter gives it to him.

9–10 *measure . . . measure:* another pun. The first means "judge." The last two mean "perform a dance."

11 *ambling:* mincing.

12 *heavy:* sad.

18 *bound:* a pun on "boundary" and "leap."

21 *pitch:* a height; therefore any distance above dull woe.

29 *case:* mask.

30 *visor for a visor:* literally "a mask for a mask." He asks for a grotesque mask to cover the grotesque mask of his face.

31 *quote:* note.

32 *beetle brows:* thick or overhanging brows of the mask.

35 *wantons:* light-hearted or playful ones.

36 *senseless rushes:* insensitive mats used to cover the floor.

37–9 *For I am . . . am done:* An old proverb warns me to keep out of the dancing. The proverb was, "Stop, while the game is fair." Romeo puns on *fair* ("at its height" and "light") and on *done* ("finished" and "drab").

40 *dun's the mouse:* Mercutio puns on Romeo's "done." The idiom means, "Be quiet."

41 *Dun:* a horse in a game called "Dun is in the mire." It was a Christmas game in which a heavy log representing Dun was placed in the center of the room and had to be lifted by the players.

42 *sir-reverence:* from the Latin salve-reverentia, save-reverence. The expression was used as a substitute for an improper or obscene word. Mercutio puns, "If you are Dun ['the horse' or 'finished'], we'll pull you from the mud of this obscene love."

43 *burn daylight:* waste time.

46 *good:* right.

47 *that:* refers to "right meaning"; *five wits:* five faculties or senses.

43–7 Mercutio says, "We delay [burn daylight]." Romeo says, "No, we don't," meaning "It's nighttime." Mercutio explains the figure of speech that he used and says it is better to understand his figurative meaning (good meaning) because it shows five times more good sense (judgment) than does understanding merely literal meaning.

49 *tonight:* last night.

53 *Queen Mab:* A fairy queen in Celtic literature.

55 *agate stone:* a gem stone in a ring. Tiny figures were often carved in the stone.

57 *atomies:* atom or mote; therefore, tiny.

59 *spinners':* spiders'.

61 *traces:* harness.

65 *worm:* An old superstition was that worms bred in the fingers of the idle.

68 *joiner:* cabinet maker.

70 *state:* pomp, as a queen travels in state.

78 *suit:* a pun on suit (clothes) and suit (plea). Courtiers often made good fees by carrying persons' pleas to court.

79 *tithe-pig's:* of the tenth pig born. Parsons were entitled to a tithe, or one-tenth, of all a parishioner's property as tax.

81 *benefice:* a good deed or a position with an assured income.

84 *ambuscadoes:* ambushes.

89 *plats:* plaits or tangles.

90 *elf-locks:* matted knots of hair in horses' manes or on human heads. The belief was that elfs caused these knots.

106 *misgives:* has misgivings, forbodes.

107 *consequences:* future events brought about by the stars. See note to line 6, Scene one.

108 *date:* time.

109 *expire:* end. Romeo speaks of ending the term of his life as though it were the end of his lease on life.

ACT ONE, SCENE FIVE

2 *trencher:* wooden platter.

7 *joint-stools:* stools made by a joiner, or cabinet maker.

7–8 *court-cupboard:* sideboard.

9 *marchpane:* almond and sugar candy molded into an ornamental shape; marzipan.

14 *great chamber:* a large common room in the homes of wealthy Elizabethans. The room could be used as a large dining room, and with the tables turned up (stood up against the walls) it could be used as a ball room.

16 *the longer liver take all:* the one who outlives or outlasts the others gets all that is left.

18 *walk a bout:* cut a caper, dance a figure.

21 *makes dainty:* makes a shy refusal.

22 *Am I come near ye now?:* Did I hit the mark? Am I close to home?

23 *Welcome gentlemen:* addressed to Romeo, Mercutio and their followers.

28 *A hall:* Make the room into a hall for dancing.

29 *turn the tables up:* See note to line 14 *supra.*

30 *quench the fire:* This fire is in conflict with the fact that it is August 1st (see note to line 14, Scene three). Perhaps Shakespeare was thinking of the Easter season of Brooke's poem or perhaps, when writing the scene, he simply envisioned the Elizabethan hall with its great fireplace. Such minor conflicts frequently occur in Shakespeare's plays. Perhaps he considered minute consistency of detail a trivial matter.

31 *unlooked for sport:* Perhaps Capulet is referring to the

appearance of the uninvited guests who relieved the monotony of the "ancient feast."

38 *Pentecost:* a church feast occurring in late spring.

40 *elder:* older than twenty-five years.

49 *dear:* a play on words: *Dear* means "precious" (as metal), "sweet," and "expensive."

56 *by his voice:* Tybalt apparently recognizes Romeo's voice.

58 *antic:* fantastic. He is masked.

59 *fleer:* mock or sneer; *solemnity:* festivity or celebration.

68 *portly:* dignified, carrying himself well.

75 *Show a fair presence:* show a happy face.

77 *It fits:* My frown is fitting.

79 *goodman boy:* a doubly insulting phrase. A *goodman* was a man who ranked below a gentleman. *go to:* an expression of impatience: "Be off with you."

81 *God shall mend my soul:* "God bless my soul," another expression of impatience.

83 *set cock-a-hoop:* start a riot. Originally the phrase meant to pull the cork out of a barrel and let the wine flow freely.

86 *trick:* trick or habit of starting quarrels; *scathe:* harm.

87 *contrary:* oppose or cross.

88 *my hearts:* my hearties. During his talk with Tybalt, Capulet is also conscious of his position as host. He addresses the dancers and gives orders to the servants. *princox:* impertinent youth.

91 *Patience perforce:* Enforced patience.

92 *different greeting:* opposition. In lines 91 and 92 Tybalt says that enforced patience in opposition with his anger (choler) makes his flesh tremble.

99 *pilgrim:* Romeo was probably costumed as a pilgrim. Thus his approach to Juliet is as a pilgrim to a shrine.

102 *palmers:* another term for a pilgrim. Actually, a palmer was a pilgrim who had been to the Holy Land. He carried a palm as a sign that he made such a pilgrimage.

107 *Saints . . . prayers' sake:* Saints do not take the initiative (move) in helping us, but will grant our requests if we pray to them.

111 *urged:* argued.

112 *You kiss by the book:* according to rules or with bookish phrases.

119 *chinks:* money.

120 *dear:* again in the double sense of "expensive" and "lovely"; *my life is my foe's debt:* my life is owed to my enemy. Juliet is now his life.

121 *the sport is at the best:* the fun has reached its high point. It is time to leave since what follows will be anti-climactic.

124 *trifling foolish banquet towards:* a little insignificant supper awaiting.

128 *fay:* faith.

130 *What:* Who.

141 *Too early seen unknown, and known too late:* I saw him too soon, before I knew who he was, and I knew who he was too late (to stop from falling in love with him).

142 *Prodigious:* Portentious, Unnatural.

ACT TWO, PROLOGUE

1 *old desire:* Romeo's love for Rosaline.

3 *fair:* fair one, namely, Rosaline.

4 *matched:* compared.

6 *alike:* equally.

10 *use to swear:* one in the habit of swearing.

13 *passion:* strong feeling.

14 *Temp'ring extremities:* modifying differences.

ACT TWO, SCENE ONE

2 *dull earth:* Romeo's body; *centre:* Juliet. In the figure of speech Romeo refers to his earth (body) finding the center of the universe (Juliet).

6 *conjure:* call up a spirit by magic.

11 *gossip:* intimate friend.

12 *purblind:* very blind.

13 *Abraham Cupid:* Eighteenth-century scholars seemed to think that Shakespeare meant Adam Cupid, after Adam Bell, a famous archer in an old ballad. Abraham, which is another form of "auburn," may refer to Cupid's hair.

14 *King Cophetua:* a character from an old ballad called "King Cophetua and the Beggar Maid." Cupid wounds the King with his arrow and causes the king to fall in love with a beggar maid at first sight.

16 *The ape is dead:* Romeo, as does a trained monkey, plays dead.

20 *demesnes:* regions.

25 *strange:* distant or belonging to another.

27 *spite:* outrage or annoyance.

28 *fair and honest:* proper and chaste, as opposed to the

obscene implications of the five previous lines of his speech.

34 *medlar:* the fruit of the *Mespilus germanica,* which can be eaten only when it is slightly rotten. A medlar is a play on "meddle," which meant "to have sexual intercourse." The fruit turns out to be a poperin pear. All of this is a part of Mercutio's obscene figure of speech.

38 *et cetera:* can be read "so and so."

38 *poperin pear:* a pear from the Flemish town of Pope-ringhe, but a slang term for the male genital organs.

39 *truckle bed:* a trundle bed. It was a bed on castors, which could be shoved under a larger bed. It was used by children or personal servants.

ACT TWO, SCENE TWO

4 *envious moon:* The moon is also Diana, goddess of chastity and virginity.

7 *Be not her maid:* Be not a follower of the virgin Diana.

8 *vestal:* virginal; *sick:* of a sick color, melancholy.

9 *fools do wear it:* court fools often wore green costumes.

17 *spheres:* heavenly bodies were thought to be contained in transparent concentric spheres that revolved around the earth.

33 *wherefore:* why, often misread as "where." This, of course, completely changes the meaning of the line. Juliet is saying, "Why are you Romeo?" It is his name that causes the problem.

39 *Thou . . . Montague:* You are yourself, even if you were not a Montague.

46 *owes:* owns.

47 *doff:* put off, discard.

53 *counsel:* intimate thoughts.

55 *dear saint:* as he addressed her in their previous meeting.

61 *if either thee dislike:* if either displease thee.

66 *o'er perch:* fly over and perch beyond.

73 *proof:* protected by armor; hence invulnerable.

76 *And but:* If only.

78 *prorogued:* postponed; *wanting of:* lacking.

88 *Fain:* Gladly; *dwell on form:* follow convention.

89 *compliment:* ceremony, polite behavior.

98 *fond:* foolish or doting.

99 *light:* unmaidenly.

101 *strange:* distant or reserved.

110 *orb:* sphere. See line 17 *supra.*

117 *contract:* betrothal.

118 *unadvised:* unthought-out, heedless.

131 *frank:* generous or liberal.

143 *thy bent of love:* the purpose of your love.

145 *procure:* cause.

152 *By and by:* Right away.

159 *falconer's:* of one who trains hawks to hunt birds.

160 *tassel-gentle:* the male hawk.

161 *Bondage . . . aloud:* Being confined, my voice is hoarse and I must speak softly.

173 *still:* always.

178 *wanton's:* spoiled child's.

180 *gyves:* fetter or shackles.

189 *ghostly:* spiritual.

190 *hap:* luck or fortune.

ACT TWO, SCENE THREE

3 *fleckeled:* spotted or streaked.

4 *Titan's:* Helios was the sun god. He was a son of Hyperion and one of the race of Titans, the early gods who inhabited Mount Olympus. Often Helios was simply referred to as Titan.

7 *osier-cage:* wicker basket.

14 *None but for some:* Even though all are not for some excellent virtue, all are for some purpose.

15 *mickle:* great; *grace:* source of divine help, power of goodness.

19 *strained:* pulled away from.

20 *Revolts from true birth:* Turns against its birthright.

25 *For this . . . each part:* the flower being smelled with the nose cheers each part of the body.

26 *with the heart:* by destroying the heart.

28 *rude will:* crude desire, lust.

30 *canker:* cankerworm, an insect that eats flowers.

31 *Benedicite:* Bless you.

33 *distempered:* disordered, diseased. The word refers to the upsetting of the humors in the body. See note to line 147, Act one, Scene one.

37 *unstuffed:* not overloaded, another reference to the humors.

50–1 *one hath . . . by me wounded:* Juliet has wounded him with Cupid's arrow as he has wounded her.

52 *physic:* remedy, healing powers.

54 *steads my foe:* aids my enemy. His plea will help Juliet (an enemy Capulet) as well as himself. Obviously, he wants the Friar to marry them.

55 *homely in thy drift:* simple in your meaning.

56 *shrift:* absolution. "Shrift" refers to both the act of confession and to the absolution, or forgiveness, obtained. Here it is obviously used in the latter sense.

60 *And all . . . must combine:* All is combined (agreed upon), except what you must combine (in marriage).

72 *To season . . . not taste:* Tears are shed for love (to salt it) but it has not the taste of the seasoning. In other words the tears do not help love.

79 *sentence:* maxim.

81 *chid'st:* scolded.

88 *by rote:* by mechanical memory. Friar Laurence says that Rosaline knew Romeo's love was mere formalized expression.

93 *stand on:* insist on.

ACT TWO, SCENE FOUR

11 *dared:* challenged.

15 *pin:* a peg at the center of a target.

16 *butt-shaft:* an unbarbed arrow with a blunt end. It was used for target practice. Mercutio says that Cupid needed only this target arrow to dispatch Romeo.

20 *Prince of Cats:* Tibert was a cat in the beast epic of *Reynard the Fox.* "Tybalt" is another form of the name.

21 *captain of compliments:* a master of polite behavior. There is also a pun here since a "compliment," in dueling, was a correct defense for a thrust.

21–2 *as you sing prick-song:* the melody that accompanied a song. It was pricked out, or written, on sheets. Tybalt's dueling was not improvised but followed a strict melody. *proportion:* rhythm.

23 *minim rests:* rests equal to half-notes.

24 *butcher of a silk button:* able to hit a button on his opponent's doublet.

25–6 *the very first house:* finest school of fencing. Mercutio is mocking Tybalt's skill with the newly popular rapier. See note to line 82, Act one Scene cne.

26 *first and second cause:* the causes for issuing a challenge according to the total code of honor. Tybalt was quick to take away cause.

27 *passado:* a forward thrust; *punto reverso:* a backhand

thrust; *the hay:* the home thrust. All three terms are from the Italian.

29 *pox:* plague; *fantasticoes:* dandies, affected persons.

30 *new turners of accent:* users of current jargon.

31 *tall:* brave.

33 *grandsire:* grandfather; addressed to Benvolio.

34 *flies:* water flies, used as a term for flatterers.

36 *form:* means "fashion" or "bench."

37 *bones:* play on English "bones" and French "bons."

39 *Without his roe, like a dried herring:* "Roe" is a short form of "Rosaline" (pronounced Rose-a-line). It is also the first sound of Romeo's name. Lastly it is used to indicate the sperm or testes (soft roe) of a male fish. Therefore, the pun runs thus: Without Rosaline he is nothing. Without his Ro, Meo (a sigh) is left. Without his roe, he is an emasculated fish.

41 *numbers:* verses; *Petrarch:* Italian sonnet writer. He dedicated his sonnets to his beloved Laura.

43 *Dido:* Queen of Carthage and beloved of Aeneas. When he abandoned her, she killed herself.

44 *Hero:* priestess of Aphrodite (Venus). Her lover Leander swam the Hellespont nightly to visit her. When he was drowned, she threw herself into the sea. *hildings:* good-for-nothings.

45 *Thisbe:* lover of Pyramus. They made love through a chink in the wall of her orchard. Their love, too, ended tragically. Shakespeare tells the story comically in a scene of *A Midsummer Night's Dream.*

47 *French slop:* baggy trousers.

51 *The slip:* A counterfeit coin was called a "slip" and getting away from someone was then called, as it is still today, "giving someone the slip."

57 *bow in the hams:* squat.

59 *kindly:* naturally.

61 *pink of courtesy:* perfection in manners.

64 *pump well flowered:* my shoe is pinked with a pattern of flowers. It is possible that Romeo here playfully kicked Mercutio. In other words if Mercutio is a flower, Romeo's shoe is flowered by kicking him.

67 *soley singular:* In two ways: (1) one sole left; (2) left markedly alone.

70 *O single . . . the singleness:* O, weak joke, outstanding for its feebleness.

73–4 *Switch and spurs . . . cry a match:* Go faster, go faster; or I'll claim a victory. A horseman would use his switch and spurs to urge on his mount. Romeo is in effect saying, "You'll have to be faster in your wit to keep up with me."

75 *wild-goose chase:* a race in which the leading horseman had to be followed in everything he did by the other horsemen in race.

76 *wild goose:* Here the phrase means "a silly person."

80 *Was I with you there for the goose?:* Did I prove you a goose?

84 *sweeting:* a kind of apple.

85 *sweet goose:* a popular dish of the time was goose and apple sauce.

86 *cheveril:* kid-leather; therefore, pliable.

87 *ell:* 45 inches.

89 *broad:* widely known, evident.

96 *natural:* a half-wit, a simpleminded person.

97 *bauble:* a fool's stick with a doll's head on the top of it. Mercutio is being obscene again.

99–100 *against the hair:* against the grain.

101 *Large:* licentious.

108 *goodly gear:* good stuff. He sees the nurse and Peter.

109 *a shirt and a smock:* a man and a woman.

116 *good den:* good evening.

119 *prick:* point. The obscenity of this pun even shocks the earthy nurse.

120 *Out upon you:* an expression of her indignation.

123 *By my troth:* In truth.

129 *fault:* want.

133 *I desire some confidence:* the nurse tries to be elegant in her language. She means conference.

135 *indite:* invite. Benvolio deliberately used the malapropism to mock the nurse.

136 *A bawd:* A procuress; *So ho:* the hunter's cry when he sights a hare.

139 *hare:* a slang term for a prostitute. *Lenten pie:* made during Lent, hence meatless.

140 *hoar:* "moldy," with a pun on "whore."

150–1 *Lady, lady, lady:* the refrain from the old ballad "Chaste Susanna."

153 *saucy merchant:* a rude fellow.

154 *ropery:* knavery.

160 *Jacks:* knaves.

161 *flirt-gills:* loose women; *skains-mates:* an unprincipled person.

181 *weak:* shifty.

183 *protest:* vow.

187 *mark:* pay attention.

201 *tackled stair:* rope ladder.

202 *top-gallant:* highest point. The top-gallant is the small mast on top of the main and fore masts of a sailing ship.

203 *convoy:* conveyance.

204 *quit thy pain:* reward your efforts.

208 *secret:* trustworthy.

209 *Two . . . away:* Two can keep a secret if only one of them knows it.

212 *prating:* chattering.

213–4 *fain lay knife abroad:* steal something by force. This is merely her picturesque way of saying that Paris wants to marry Juliet.

214 *lief:* willingly.

216 *properer:* handsomer.

218 *clout:* dishrag; *versal:* universal.

220 *a letter:* the same letter.

223 *that's the dog's name:* The letter *R*, because it sounds like a growl, was called the "dog letter." Actually the nurse, who was undoubtedly illiterate, did not realize that the sound rō (Romeo and rosemary) was formed with an *r*.

225 *sententious:* the nurse's mistake for "sentences" or "maxims."

226 *rosemary:* a shrub that symbolized remembrance. The nurse is saying, "Juliet is writing the prettiest sentence about you and remembrance."

232 *Before, and apace:* Go before me and quickly.

ACT TWO, SCENE FIVE

6 *louring:* lowering and frowning.

7 *nimble-pinioned doves draw love:* light-winged doves were usually depicted pulling the chariot of Venus (love).

14 *bandy:* to hit back and forth as a tennis ball is hit; therefore to drive quickly.

16 *feign:* carry themselves.

21 *sad:* serious.

26 *jaunce:* jaunt, hard trip.

36 *stay the circumstance:* wait for the details. We still use a similar expression, "Under the circumstances," to mean conditions or details.

38 *simple:* simpleminded, silly.

52 *Beshrew:* curse.

64 *come up:* an expression of impatience like, "Come off it" or "Go to."

67 *coil:* fuss.

72 *Now . . . cheeks:* Now you begin to blush.

ACT TWO, SCENE SIX

4 *countervail:* counterbalance.

10 *like fire and powder:* Cannon were discharged by applying fire to loose powder.

12 *Is loathsome in his own deliciousness:* Becomes distasteful when overeaten.

15 *Too swift arrives as tardy as too slow:* Going too fast will make you just as late as going too slow.

17 *everlasting flint:* perhaps the stone floor of the Friar's cell.

18 *gossamers:* cobweb threads.

20 *vanity:* foolishness or dizziness, i.e., of love.

21 *ghostly:* spiritual.

23 *As much . . . too much:* The same greeting to him; i.e., good even, or else if it isn't, his thanks are too much

25 *that:* if that.

26 *blazon:* proclaim.

28 *Unfold:* Make known.

30 *Conceit:* Imagination, or Understanding.

32 *worth:* wealth.

ACT THREE, SCENE ONE

8 *by the operation of the second cup:* when the second drink begins to work on him.

9 *drawer:* the boy who brings the drinks in the tavern; a waiter.

13–4 *as soon moved to be moody, and as soon moody to be moved:* as inclined to get angry as he is angry when crossed.

33 *tutor me from quarrelling:* teach me how not to quarrel.

35 *fee-simple:* absolute ownership, a legal phrase; *an hour and a quarter:* a small fraction of the day, hence, cheaply.

48 *consortest:* keep company.

49 *consort:* Mercutio uses it here as combining to make musical harmony.

51 *fiddlestick:* rapier.

59 *my man:* the man I'm looking for. Mercutio deliberately twists it to meaning "my servant."

61 *field:* here used as a place for a duel.

66 *appertaining:* rightful or suitable.

68 *knowest me not:* He does not know that Romeo is now his kinsman by his marriage to Juliet.

69 *Boy:* a term of insult.

72 *devise:* think.

74 *tender:* regard or cherish.

77 *Alla stoccata carries it away:* A direct thrust wins the day. Mercutio means that Tybalt's bold insults have caused Romeo to back down.

78 *rat-catcher:* reference to his being King of Cats. See note to line 20, Act two, Scene four; *will you walk:* a phrase challenging him to fight; similar to the phrase in our Western movies, "I'm calling you out."

81 *make bold withal:* take liberties with.

82 *dry-beat:* beat without drawing blood. Mercutio says he will take one of his nine lives and, if his manners are not improved, he will beat to death the other eight lives.

84 *pilcher:* scabbard.

88 *passado:* a thrust. See note to line 27, Act two, Scene four.

90 *forbear:* stop.

92 *bandying:* fighting.

94 *sped:* finished.

101–2 *grave man:* Mercutio makes his last pun even though mortally wounded; *peppered:* finished.

106 *book of arithmetic:* by the rules set down in a book on fencing.

114 *ally:* kinsman.

122 *aspired:* risen to.

124 *on more days doth depend:* more days cast a shadow.

128 *respective lenity:* thoughtful gentleness.

129 *conduct:* guide or leader.

139 *amazed:* stunned; *doom:* condemn.

141 *fortune's fool:* the plaything of fortune.

147 *discover:* reveal.

148 *manage:* management or conduct.

158 *spoke him fair:* spoke to him civilly.

159 *nice:* trivial.

162 *take . . . spleen:* make peace with the wild anger.

163 *tilts:* strikes.

169 *Retorts:* Throws back.

173 *envious:* hateful.

174 *stout:* stout-hearted, brave.

175 *by and by:* at once.

176 *entertained:* considered.

182 *affection:* friendship.

194 *My blood:* Mercutio was the Prince's kinsman.

195 *amerce:* punish by a fine.

198 *purchase out abuses:* redeem or buy off misdeeds.

201 *attend our will:* wait on my judgment.

ACT THREE, SCENE TWO

2 *Phoebus:* Apollo, god of light, often confused with Helios, the sun god, who drew the fiery sun across the sky each day with his chariot.

3 *Phaethon:* son of the sun god, here Phoebus, who stole his father's chariot and attempted to drive the sun across the heaven. He could not hold the reins and the runaway team threatened to destroy the world. Zeus, to prevent this, killed Phaethon with a thunderbolt.

6 *runaway's eyes may wink:* a very controversial phrase. The "runaway" is probably Phaethon. Juliet asks that the eyes of day close (wink) so that it will be night.

10 *civil:* refined or courteous.

12 *learn:* teach.

14 *Hood:* Cover; a term from falconry. A hood was placed over the head of an excited falcon in order to calm him down. *unmanned:* untamed, again from falconry. *bating:* fluttering, again from falconry.

15 *strange:* reserved or shy.

46 *I:* ay. Even Juliet uses word play.

47 *cockatrice:* a mythological serpent that was supposed to be able to kill at a glance.

49 *those eyes:* Romeo's, and the conclusion of Juliet's pun on *ay, I,* and *eye.*

53 *God save the mark:* an oath to keep off bad luck.

54 *corse:* corpse.

56 *gore-blood:* clotted blood; *swounded:* swooned. The nurse again mixes up a word.

59 *Vile earth, to earth resign:* The vile earth is her body. She demands it to be committed to earth and buried.

67 *dreadful trumpet:* the trumpet that heralds the end of the world; *general doom:* day of judgment.

73-9 These lines are filled with oxymoron (see note on to

lines 177–82, Act one Scene one). The bittersweet images express Juliet's ambivalence toward Romeo.

81 *bower:* give lodging to.

87 *forsworn:* faithless. One who forswears is a breaker of vows.

88 *aqua-vitae:* spirits, liquor.

117 *needly:* necessarily.

120 *modern:* ordinary.

121 *rearward:* rear guard. She puns on "ward," which is pronounced as "word," and picks up "word" again in her next line.

139 *wot:* know.

ACT THREE, SCENE THREE

1 *fearful:* full of fear.

4 *doom:* judgment.

10 *vanished:* issued.

20 *world's exile:* exile from the world.

26 *rushed aside:* thrust violently aside.

28 *dear:* important, worthy, extraordinary.

33 *validity:* value.

34 *courtship:* a pun; he means both "courtliness" and "pursuit of love."

45 *mean of death:* means of death; *so mean:* so bare.

52 *fond:* foolish.

59 *Displant:* Remove.

63 *Let me dispute with thee of thy estate:* Let me discuss reasonably with you your circumstances.

77 *simpleness:* foolishness.

84 *even:* exactly.

85 *woeful sympathy:* Romeo and Juliet feel their sorrow together.

90 *O:* a sigh or exclamation of grief.

94 *old:* established, hardened.

98 *concealed:* The fact that she is married to Romeo is concealed to the world.

103 *level:* aim.

106 *anatomy:* body.

113 *Or ill-beseeming beast in seeming both:* Oh shameful beast in appearing to be both man and woman.

115 *tempered:* blended or mixed.

126 *form of wax:* a dummy. The nurse used "man of wax"

to describe Paris's beauty. (See note to line 76, Act one, Scene three.) Friar Laurence is not impressed with external parts.

134 *And thou dismembered with thine own defence:* And you blown up with your own gun powder.

137 *There art thou happy:* In that you are lucky.

148 *watch:* guard.

151 *blaze:* proclaim; *your friends:* families.

157 *apt:* inclined.

166 *here stands all your state:* everything depends on what I'm going to tell you now.

174 *so brief:* so quickly.

ACT THREE, SCENE FOUR

1 *fall'n out:* happened or resulted.

2 *move:* make your proposal to.

11 *mewed up:* cooped up, a term from falconry.

12 *desperate tender:* bold offer.

16 *my son:* Paris, of course, will be his son-in-law.

24 *late:* lately.

25 *held him carelessly:* cared not enough for him.

32 *against:* in anticipation of.

34 *Afore me:* Most scholars think this phrase a mild oath like "before God." The phrase may, however, be a command by Capulet to Paris or to the torchbearers to precede him.

ACT THREE, SCENE FIVE

8 *lace:* ornament, stripe; *severing:* breaking up.

9 *Night's candles:* the stars.

13 *exhales:* Meteors were thought to be formed by fiery gases sucked up and "exhaled" by the sun.

20 *reflex of Cynthia's brow:* reflection of the moon. Cynthia, (a Renaissance name for Diana) was often depicted with a crescent moon on her forehead.

23 *care:* desire.

28 *sharps:* shrill notes.

29 *division:* musical variety.

31 *change eyes:* The toad has bright eyes and an ugly voice; the lark has ugly eyes and a lovely voice.

33 *affray:* frighten.

34 *hunt's-up:* an early-morning cry used to arouse huntsmen.

54 *ill divining:* evil-foreboding [in my].

59 *Dry sorrow drinks our blood:* A popular belief of the time was that sighing and sorrow caused the blood to descend to the bowels, where the heat sucked up the heart's blood, thus causing paleness.

67 *down:* abed.

68 *procures her:* causes her to come.

75 *feeling:* heartfelt.

84 *like he:* as much as he.

90 *runagate:* a renegade or vagabond.

91 *unaccustomed dram:* strange dose.

95 *dead:* Can be read with the line that precedes it or the line that follows it. Juliet is deliberately equivocating here.

98 *temper:* Again Juliet equivocates. She knows her mother will take the word to mean "mix" but she means "modify."

102 *wreak:* (1) to revenge; (2) to gratify.

110 *sorted out:* chosen.

112 *in happy time:* a vague phrase that can have several meanings. Here it seems to mean "indeed" or "by the way."

130 *conduit:* fountain or water pipe.

132 *Thou counterfeits a bark:* You imitate a boat.

140 *will none:* refuses.

142 *Soft, take me with you:* Wait a minute, let me understand you.

145 *wrought:* procured.

150 *chop-logic:* one who argues with oversubtle distinctions, a hairsplitter.

152 *minion:* a darling or pet child.

154 *fettle:* make ready.

156 *hurdle:* a wooden cart on which prisoners were carried to execution.

157 *green sickness carrion:* pale piece of flesh. Green-sickness was a kind of anemia that made young girls pale.

165 *My fingers itch:* He wants to strike her.

169 *hilding:* good for nothing, wretch.

170 *rate:* berate, scold.

172 *smatter:* chatter.

173 *O God ye god-den:* God give you good evening. He is dismissing her.

175 *Utter your gravity o'er a gossip's bowl:* Speak your wisdom over a punch bowl.

177 *God's bread:* an oath on the Blessed Sacrament.

182 *demesnes:* estates.

183 *parts:* qualities.

185 *puling:* whining.

186 *mammet:* doll, puppet; *in her fortunes tender:* in the offer of good fortune that she has received.

189 *I'll pardon you:* read sarcastically.

191 *I do not use to jest:* I am not used to making jokes.

192 *advise:* be advised.

197 *be forsworn:* break my oath.

207 *my faith in heaven:* my marriage vow is recorded in heaven.

211 *practise stratagems:* play violent tricks.

215 *all the world to nothing:* The nurse quotes odds. The phrase is like saying, "It's a million to one."

216 *challenge:* claim.

219 *county:* The count Paris.

222 *green:* Green eyes were much admired; *quick:* lively.

223 *Beshrew:* curse.

227 *here:* on this earth.

235 *Ancient damnation:* You damned old woman.

236 *forsworn:* breaking my vow to Romeo.

ACT FOUR, SCENE ONE

2 *father:* future father-in-law.

3 *nothing slow to slack his haste:* not so slow as to slow him down.

10 *That she do give her sorrow so much sway:* That she gives way to grief too much.

13 *minded by herself alone:* only in the case of herself; too much alone.

40 *entreat the time alone:* ask that you leave us alone.

41 *shield:* forbid.

47 *compass of my wits:* limits of my intelligence.

48 *prorogue:* postpone.

54 *presently:* at once.

57 *label:* a seal on a legal document; *deed:* a certificate of ownership. Juliet says that before she will put her hand to a false document (marriage to Paris) she will kill herself.

62 *extremes:* straits or difficulties.

63 *arbitrating:* judging or deciding.

64 *commission:* authority.

75 *cop'st:* contends or vies.

79 *thievish ways:* highways that robbers frequent.

81 *charnel house:* a human bone house. Graves were used over and over. Old bones were dug up and deposited in the charnel house.

83 *reeky:* reeking or stinking; *chapless:* jawless.
94 *distilling:* permeating.
97 *surcease:* shall stop.
100 *waned:* pale.
102 *supple government:* control of movement.
110 *uncovered:* with face exposed.
113 *against:* in anticipation of.
114 *drift:* purpose.
119 *toy:* whim or fancy.

ACT FOUR, SCENE TWO

6–7 *'tis an ill cook that cannot lick his own fingers:* Only a poor cook won't eat his own cooking.
10 *unfurnished:* unprepared.
14 *peevish:* silly; *harlotry:* hussy.
26 *becomed:* fitting, proper.
33 *closet:* private room.
34 *sort:* select.
35 *furnish:* fit out.
38 *provision:* supplies.
45 *prepare up:* prepare thoroughly.

ACT FOUR, SCENE THREE

3 *orisons:* prayers.
5 *cross:* perverse.
8 *behoveful:* needed; *state:* ceremony.
15 *faint:* causing faintness.
25 *ministered:* administered.
29 *tried:* proved, shown by trial.
36 *like:* likely.
37 *conceit:* idea or imagining.
42 *green in earth:* recently buried.
47 *mandrakes:* roots of a mandragora plant. The roots were used as a narcotic. The plant, shaped like a human, was supposed to shriek when pulled up and cause madness to the hearer.
53 *rage:* madness.
58 *stay:* stop. Juliet imagines that she sees Tybalt trying to kill Romeo.

ACT FOUR, SCENE FOUR

2 *pastry:* room where the pastry is made.

4 *curfew bell:* originally a name for the evening bell. Later it was applied to other ringings.

5 *baked meats:* pies and pastries including meat pies.

6 *cot-queen:* a man too concerned with household affairs. Notice the familiarity with which the Nurse addresses Capulet. She obviously had great freedom in the household.

8 *watching:* staying awake.

11 *mouse-hunt:* a slang phrase meaning "woman-hunter."

13 *Jealous-hood:* A woman's jealousy; perhaps, because she wore a hood.

19 *Mass:* by the Mass; *whoreson:* literally, "a bastard," but used in a good-natured sense to mean "fellow."

20 *logger-head:* blockhead.

ACT FOUR, SCENE FIVE

1 *Fast:* fast asleep.

2 *you slug-a-bed:* you sleepy-head.

4 *pennyworths:* little naps.

6 *set up his rest:* resolved. The phrase is from a card game called "primero."

26 *settled:* congealed.

40 *living:* livelihood and property.

43 *unhappy:* fatal.

60 *Uncomfortable:* Joyless.

61 *solemnity:* festive celebration.

65 *Confusion's:* Destruction's. The word is played off on the modern sense of the word in the next line.

72 *advanced:* exalted, played off against "advanced" in the next line.

83 *nature's tears are reason's merriment:* Our emotions make us feel sad about things that reason tells us are good. The Friar apparently speaks of the fact that Juliet's soul has gone to heaven. He really knows, of course, that she still lives.

87 *cheer:* feast.

99 *case:* The nurse means "situation." The musician means "cover" (for his instrument).

101 *heart's ease:* a popular tune of the day.

108 *dump:* sad tune.

115 *gleek:* jest, mocking.

116 *the minstrel:* apparently intended as some sort of insult, although the term is not known in this sense today.

120 *carry no crotchets:* put up with none of your fancy no-

tions. Crotchets were also musical quarter-notes.

122 *note:* a pun: (1) notice, (2) put me to music.

128–30 *When . . . sound:* from a song by Richard Edwards, published in the *Paradyse of Daynty Devises* (1576).

132 *Catling:* a small lute made of catgut. The surnames of musicians indicated their professions.

135 *Rebeck:* a fiddle with three strings.

137 *Soundpost:* a small peg that supports the body of a stringed instrument.

141 *cry you mercy:* beg your pardon.

144 *sounding:* playing.

147 *pestilent:* pesty, bothersome.

150 *stay:* remain for.

ACT FIVE, SCENE ONE

1–2 *If . . . hand:* If I can trust my dreams, I'm about to receive good news.

3 *bosom's lord:* heart.

7 *gives a dead man leave:* allows a dead man.

11 *shadows:* phantoms or images.

21 *took post:* hired a post horse.

23 *office:* duty.

24 *I defy you, stars:* another reference to fate. Here Romeo will decide his own fate.

39 *weeds:* clothing. We still use the term "widow's weeds." *overwhelming:* overhanging.

40 *Culling:* sorting; *simples:* medicinal herbs.

45 *beggarly account:* meager amount.

47 *packthread:* twine used for tying parcels; *cakes of roses:* small cakes of dried rose petals.

52 *caitiff:* miserable.

59 *ducats:* coins, usually gold, of various values.

60 *dram:* drink; *gear:* matter.

63 *trunk:* body.

66 *mortal:* deadly.

67 *any he:* any man; *utters:* circulates or sells.

85 *cordial:* a heart stimulant.

ACT FIVE, SCENE TWO

4 *mind:* thoughts.

6 *associate:* accompany.

8 *searchers:* officials who check on sanitary conditions and report of plague.

18 *nice:* trivial; *charge:* weight.

19 *dear import:* great importance.

21 *crow:* crowbar.

26 *accidents:* events.

ACT FIVE, SCENE THREE

3 *lay thee all along:* lie at full length.

14 *sweet water:* perfumed water.

16 *obsequies:* ceremonies performed in honor of the dead.

20 *cross:* thwart.

21 *Muffle:* Hide.

22 *mattock:* pickaxe.

33 *jealous:* suspicious.

39 *empty:* hungry.

41 *Take thou that:* Romeo gives him a purse of money.

45 *maw:* stomach.

48 *despite:* scorn.

56 *apprehend:* arrest, seize.

68 *conjurations:* entreaties.

77 *attend:* listen to.

83 *triumphant:* splendid.

84 *lantern:* a tower with many windows. Romeo says that Juliet's grave is such a tower.

86 *feasting presence:* festive chamber where a king appears on occasions of state.

89 *keepers:* nurses.

90 *lightning:* last surge of life.

96 *advanced:* raised.

105 *paramour:* lover.

110 *set up my everlasting rest:* remain forever.

115 *dateless bargain to engrossing death:* Eternal agreement with monopolizing death.

116 *conduct:* leader.

121 *speed:* bring me here on time.

122 *stumbled at graves:* a bad omen.

142 *masterless:* discarded by their owners.

148 *comfortable:* able to give comfort.

162 *timeless:* untimely.

163 *churl:* miser.

165 *Haply:* Perhaps.

166 *restorative:* Romeo's life.

169 *happy:* opportune.

173 *attach:* seize or arrest.

179 *woes:* sorrowful things.

181 *circumstance:* particulars; *descry:* discover.

203 *house:* scabbard.

207 *my old age:* Lady Capulet is not yet thirty years old. Shakespeare may have been careless here, but then again such an ordeal would make many women feel that youth is passed.

214 *manners:* The old should be allowed to pass first.

216 *Seal up the mouth of outrage:* Stop this outcry. Not only is the Prince asking them to stop the emotional outburst, but he is also directing the servants to close the tomb. On the Elizabethan stage, the bodies would be on an inner stage and with these words the curtains would be closed on them.

221 *be slave to patience:* give way to patience, i.e., bear your sorrow patiently.

222 *parties of suspicion:* the suspects, those under suspicion.

226 *impeach:* charge with crime; *purge:* clean.

229 *short date of breath:* short time to live.

238 *perforce:* by force, against his will.

247 *as this:* on this very.

253 *prefixed hour:* previously agreed upon time.

255 *closely:* secretly.

266 *privy:* aware of the secret.

270 *still:* always.

273 *post:* haste.

279 *raised:* aroused.

280 *made:* did.

293 *joys:* the two children.

295 *brace of kinsmen:* pair of relatives; i.e., Mercutio and Paris.

297 *jointure:* part of a dowry reserved for a widow.

301 *at such rate be set:* of such value.

305 *glooming:* gloomy.